The
Culturally Conscious Board

Setting the Boardroom Table for Impact

Jennifer M. Jukanovich

Russell W. West

BK

Berrett–Koehler Publishers, Inc.

Copyright © 2024 by Jennifer M. Jukanovich, PhD and Russell W. West, PhD

All rights reserved. No part of this publication may be reproduced, distributed, or transmitted in any form or by any means, including photocopying, recording, or other electronic or mechanical methods, without the prior written permission of the publisher, except in the case of brief quotations embodied in critical reviews and certain other noncommercial uses permitted by copyright law. For permission requests, write to the publisher, addressed "Attention: Permissions Coordinator," at the address below.

Berrett-Koehler Publishers, Inc.
1333 Broadway, Suite 1000, Oakland, CA 94612-1921
Tel: (510) 817-2277 | Fax: (510) 817-2278, www.bkconnection.com

ORDERING INFORMATION

Quantity sales. Special discounts are available on quantity purchases by corporations, associations, and others. For details, contact the "Special Sales Department" at the Berrett-Koehler address above.

Individual sales. Berrett-Koehler publications are available through most bookstores. They can also be ordered directly from Berrett-Koehler: Tel: (800) 929-2929; Fax: (802) 864-7626; www.bkconnection.com.

Orders for college textbook/course adoption use. Please contact Berrett-Koehler: Tel: (800) 929-2929; Fax: (802) 864-7626.

Distributed to the U.S. trade and internationally by Penguin Random House Publisher Services.

Berrett-Koehler and the BK logo are registered trademarks of Berrett-Koehler Publishers, Inc.

Printed in Canada

Berrett-Koehler books are printed on long-lasting acid-free paper. When it is available, we choose paper that has been manufactured by environmentally responsible processes. These may include using trees grown in sustainable forests, incorporating recycled paper, minimizing chlorine in bleaching, or recycling the energy produced at the paper mill.

Library of Congress Cataloging-in-Publication Data
Names: Jukanovich, Jennifer M., author. | West, Russell W., author.
Title: The culturally conscious board : setting the boardroom table for impact / Jennifer M. Jukanovich, Russell W. West.
Description: First edition. | Oakland, CA : Berrett-Koehler Publishers, Inc., [2024] | Includes bibliographical references and index.
Identifiers: LCCN 2024003004 (print) | LCCN 2024003005 (ebook) | ISBN 9798890570154 (paperback) | ISBN 9798890570161 (pdf) | ISBN 9798890570178 (epub)
Subjects: LCSH: Boards of directors. | Multiculturalism.
Classification: LCC HD2745 .J853 2024 (print) | LCC HD2745 (ebook) | DDC 658.4/22—dc23/eng/20240412
LC record available at https://lccn.loc.gov/2024003004
LC ebook record available at https://lccn.loc.gov/2024003005

FIRST EDITION

32 31 30 29 28 27 26 25 24 ■ 10 9 8 7 6 5 4 3 2 1

Book production: BookMatters
Cover design: Ashley Ingram
Interior figures created by Russell W. West, PhD

To all those who use their time, talent and treasure

in service to the common good.

Your voice is needed at the boardroom table.

Contents

Foreword

Picture it with me: a group of people united around a common mission, making decisions informed by every insight in the group, for the sake of the common good. Multiple generations, skin colors, educational backgrounds and family histories represented around one table, working toward a shared vision of flourishing. Imagine a group: aware of their differences and fully valuing them; acknowledging their points of disagreement and fully embracing them. This group sees! They see one another as human—as fully human as themselves—and understand the necessity of their "sight" to do the hard task of pooling their time and talents to make the world a place where everyone can be so valued and known.

No, I'm not describing some utopian aspiration or heavenly courtroom, and yes, I have been paying attention the last few years. I know that the United States is more polarized now than it has been in decades. As Jennifer and Russ share in the following pages, the Edelman Trust Barometer reveals some alarming statistics: less than one-third of those surveyed would help someone in need who strongly disagreed with them or their point of view, and only one in five would be willing to live in the same neighborhood or have them as a coworker. These are deep, distressing and truly destructive realities that are being felt at every level of society today. Change that solves problems and increases trust positions us for long-term sustainability. It makes the image of the boardroom above critical to embrace. The image is a vision in which we can choose to believe; together, true and diverse collaboration is possible. Strong decisions that will move the needle in our communities can be made through this type of gathering. This book offers us both insight and an invitation to get there. It is timely and needed.

In the following pages, Russ and Jennifer lay out essential principles for strengthening boardroom culture that will in turn better serve communities. These pages are practical, relatable, digestible and compelling. They touch on the unspoken realities of boardroom culture that influence decisions and shape the experiences of board members. They operate on the astute observation that every board already has a culture; the question is, is it one that welcomes, affirms and creates meaningful, mission-centered change in our communities? They gently challenge some long-accepted norms that might bear reconsideration, and they share stories that help us find ourselves in their narratives so we can change the plot trajectories of our own boards. They do it all borne out of decades of board leadership experience that we at the M.J. Murdock Charitable Trust have been fortunate to learn from and pass along to hundreds of nonprofits. We are grateful to be part of the seeds that nurtured these ideas and recipients of the fruit borne from Russ's and Jennifer's work.

But above all, the wise and trustworthy authors of this book give us a vision for how to operate as a community that embraces differences for the sake of the common good. As one of our board trustees remarked, working for the common good is not so common, meaning it is not as common as it needs to be to achieve it. This is true. It is not, and in our day and age, it is more needed than ever. If our organizational leadership can model true and effective collaboration, maybe we can change the norm together so that one day, that vision of a well-functioning board would seem a little less utopic and a little more recognizable. And maybe that collaborative spirit can create islands of sanctuary in our polarized world that will spill over into every level of our organizations, our cities, our communities and our families.

Romanita Hairston, CEO, M.J. Murdock Charitable Trust

Preface

Our Invitation

Welcome to *The Culturally Conscious Board*! We, Jennifer and Russ, hope this book can help you uncover the hidden strengths of your board culture. We hope it deepens the cultural awareness of every board member. There is more to board culture than its visible and material furniture. Each of its members is dressed in distinctive cultural clothing. Each, regardless of their cosmetics and complexions, is immersed in their own orienting memberships. Each board director brings a cultural blend of values shaped by their family, language, social memberships, economic capacity, faith or no faith. These are the "garments" we wear that display our culture, whether we are conscious of it or not.

In early 2020, amid the pandemic, the M.J. Murdock Charitable Trust, a foundation vested in the transformation of more than 3,000 nonprofit organizations, reaffirmed its conviction that effective board enrichment must attend to four pillars: *governance, culture, sustainability* and *strategy*. During this period, it became increasingly apparent also that boards were struggling, sometimes failing, to match widespread anxiety in the social and political environment. Boards called for help. When seeking tools that could help boards become islands of sanctuary in this moment of social foment and division, few resources were equal to the demands. That is where the story of *The Culturally Conscious Board* begins.

Jennifer was completing a career reflection process in the form of a

PhD after years of intercultural living, service and advocacy. She was asking deeper questions about recognizing leadership among those without institutional power. She found her own leadership deeply formed by unseen and unheard voices, particularly among Rwandan women with whom she had worked for several years. And as she moved from international development to higher education leadership and served under and on numerous boards, she recognized how often those voices went unrecognized to the detriment of the mission. And what she uncovered was the importance of how crucial humility and trust are to effective leadership, no matter what strata of society.

Meanwhile, Russ, at the crest of a 30-plus-year career as a tenured graduate school professor of leadership, resigned his faculty and deanship roles to put his capacity-building know-how to work on a "wicked problem in the transformation sector."[1] He joined a gritty mission-based NGO, waist-deep in the global plight of families whose livelihoods and dignity are entangled daily in waste dump colonies. Two years into his dream job as strategy impact officer, a donor crisis cascaded into the NGO's funding crisis, which necessitated a fiscal emergency. This chain reaction left Russ on the painful receiving end of a board's necessary fiscal survival actions (sustainability actions with which he actually agrees!).

Both Jennifer and Russ, on different paths, while engaging in social impact efforts, were being forced to examine the role of forces beyond the boardroom table that weighed heavily on boardroom tables. Many of these forces were being left unlabeled or ignored, or in the worst of cases, they could not be discussed in a timely manner because of the self-silencing dynamics that could happen in any group. In addition, a mood of distrust and fatigue pervaded the wider culture, raising doubtful questions when terms like *DEI* and *cultural competency* were urged as fixes, even when some boards were unclear exactly what was broken. Because culture can be elusive, abstract cures were worse than the ailments they were meant to address. Kimberly Thornbury, senior vice president of the M.J. Murdock Charitable Trust, encouraged Jennifer and Russ to pool their lived insights from working with boards and to go deeper, perhaps in the form of a practical little book. In service to the Trust's nonprofit board leadership development program, the team responded with a more invitational approach, one meant to offer a *via media*, a "third way" amid either/or solutions. They assumed, if ever board members have enjoyed being guests, or if they have offered the dignity of welcome to others as hosts, they just might have what it takes to discover and steward their own board's culture as an asset. *The Culturally Conscious Board: Setting the Boardroom Table for Impact* is our humble invitation to deeper boards, deeper conversations, and ultimately deeper impacts for the common good.

INTRODUCTION
Every Board Has a Culture

We but mirror the world....If we could change ourselves, the tendencies in the world would also change. As a man changes his own nature, so does the attitude of the world change towards him. This is the divine mystery supreme. A wonderful thing it is and the source of our happiness. We need not wait to see what others do.

MAHATMA GANDHI[2]

Boards make decisions.

That's the job.

If you really think about it, it is your board's *only* job.

We understand if these words strike you as odd. If we were in your shoes, we might protest: "You don't know my board! They sure do seem to have lots of jobs for me—attend lots of late-night meetings, sponsor a table at the annual galas, pose for pictures in hard hats with gold spray-painted shovels, sign staff birthday cards, cajole colleagues and neighbors into also getting on board and on it goes. And you say I have but *one* job?!"

You make a very good point. Boards can be quite busy. Yet, while boards might be frequently called upon to show their support for the organizations for which they provide governance leadership, not all of these activities are the same. Boards indeed engage in varied and countless activities in their assorted roles as cheerleaders of the chief

1

executive and staff, volunteers in service with constituents, event participants and donors.

Yet, we maintain, when your chapter of board service is complete, a record of your board's deliberated decisions will be ensconced in your minutes, well, forever. More importantly, the authorizations, policies and agreements that these decisions represent will have set in motion mandates, people and acts of service that have the potential to transform the lives of real people, some of whom may be your nearest neighbors or the nations next door and beyond.

When a board makes a decision, a spark occurs in the obscurity of those late-night meetings mentioned above. A well-formed decision combusts. It ignites a chain reaction of purpose, duty and impact in the lives of everyone along its fulfillment system, including you and your colleagues. When a board is seated, deliberate in the stewardship of its authority and the execution of its duties, the world begins to change. This change emerges gradually through a staff policy or a budgetary mandate. The change is mediated through a chief executive team's execution of shared business and measured in results like the fortified attention span of a child in a classroom, who can finally concentrate because she and her siblings have a warm home, nutritious food and a parent whose generational fortunes are forever changed, simply because they walked through the doors of an agency that will remain open one more year because of your board's decision.

A board decision is a small act of service, with an exponential significance to the circle of stakeholders who depend on that decision's integrity, in some cases to survive. No board is perfect; therefore, we need not be romantic about our expectations of these human decision teams. Boards must make the best decisions within their capacity. It is to that capacity we want to draw your attention in *The Culturally Conscious Board: Setting the Boardroom Table for Impact.*

You see, we think most boards are operating at half capacity. We mean no offense in this assertion. But it's our experience. It is the

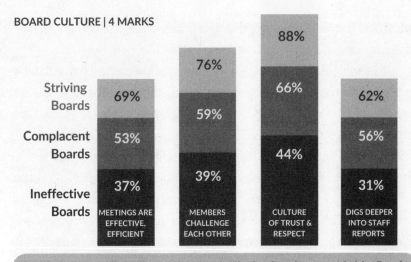

BOARD CULTURE | 4 MARKS

Striving Boards
Complacent Boards
Ineffective Boards

	MEETINGS ARE EFFECTIVE, EFFICIENT	MEMBERS CHALLENGE EACH OTHER	CULTURE OF TRUST & RESPECT	DIGS DEEPER INTO STAFF REPORTS
Striving	69%	76%	88%	62%
			66%	
Complacent	53%	59%		56%
			44%	
Ineffective	37%	39%		31%

McKinsey Survey | The difference between *Ineffective, Complacent* and *Striving Boards* is reflected in how each consciously invests in their board culture practices.

FIGURE I.1 Culture-Deepening Practices, a Comparison

reported experience of board members widely. McKinsey's board culture survey asks boards about four practices that shift board culture (Figure I.1). The differences in practice between what McKinsey labels *ineffective, complacent* and *striving* boards are sobering.[3]

When boards do poorly, organizations cannot be far behind. (Most boards have the matter reversed: "If it ever goes south, it'll be on the staff"—and by implication, not on the clean-handed board.) This evasion of responsibility is not exactly explicitly stated. But some boards, by their inattention to culture, demonstrate a fundamental misunderstanding of what it means to be on a board exactly. It can all turn into such mind-numbing administrative routine. Shuffling papers. Report parades by staff. Meandering and anxiety-provoking speeches by the founder who just cannot let go. One more roll call with 40% of the board using up their discretionary absences. Most boards are immersed in this stuff. Sure, they get things done. But the whole exercise can leave members feeling, well, half awake.

When table culture—we will get into the meaning of that later—gets reduced to only tackling agendas and approving financials, it can leave would-be loyal members wondering whether this is worth their time. When your table culture can be reduced to the sum of all the minutes, roll calls, old business and seconded motions, then that is the only level of consciousness your board expects of itself. Routine lulls into inattention. The trivial and critical get equal time. And if old-timers treat this sleep state as normal or preferred, newcomers will take their seats and settle in for their own long winter naps at your table. A veritable comfort zone of certainty and efficiency. We can believe it is all out on the table until a surprise occurs that awakens us to what is hidden in plain sight.

Hindsight tends to be 20/20, but even with hindsight, we only have interest in the lesson because consequences finally have their say. Pain has a brisk way of awakening us to what can no longer be denied. When the pain of an incomplete decision comes home to roost, then all we can do is interrogate reality. Of course, when the receipts are in, and the deed is done, it's too late. Because who really needs a great decision from a board in hindsight, when it's too late? Commentary on last week's news and last year's performance assumptions is an odd way to go forward. While no one expects boards to predict the future, it is not too much to expect a team of decision-makers to be good at their core duty.

So what if half capacity fails to capture the whole story? What if the transactional parliamentary existence that most boards live in is only the visible surface of your board's culture?

Most boards would benefit from deepening their view of board culture. The same can be said for a rediscovery of what the board means in their lives. We think a more transformational view of board service is in order. Seldom does a headline news event occur in which the mastery and malpractice of deliberative bodies is not on full display. It makes it easy to agree with "As goes the board, so goes the organization." It's hard not to ask, Where was the board? What were they thinking?

We invite boards to take stock of the moment in which we find ourselves. Mission-based, socially responsible, transformational organizations are needed more today than ever. The wheels of government worldwide give signs of real unsteadiness. In times past when big systems faltered, a social sector composed of idealistic, stubborn change agents has always emerged and steadied the cart. Sometimes philanthropists, sometimes social enterprises, sometimes scrappy faith-based relief efforts and sometimes partnerships of the oddest stripe and hue may be all that stand in the gap for some of the globe's most intractable economic, environmental, social and spiritual challenges.

We need boards who are alert to the exponential capacity they can release by digging deep into why they have gathered to govern. Status quo won't do. And when these stand-in-the-gap boards convene, we as board members around their boardroom tables are allowed to serve something greater than ourselves. We're going to need help, all kinds of new help.

Onboarding new talent to join that venture may be a challenging task under any circumstances. Add the intentionality necessary to invite people whose social identity, experience and voice may challenge the status quo and require more than cosmetic or complexion changes in the group. An inquiry into what a board is prepared to consider in its decision-making rituals may be required. Can the unmentionable be made mentionable as a matter of service to the mission? Can the cultivation and preservation of conversational space—the table—remain psychologically safe, welcoming of curiosity, serious about the ethical implications of questions the board is invited to consider? Is there solidity of character necessary to transcend differences and call things by their rightful names when your board is confronted with a question for which no conventional wisdom or rule of thumb exists?

The answer would be yes, always yes, if learning, growing, changing is built into the expectations of board participation. Collaborative, deliberative board practices must cultivate a culturally conscious mindset that critiques the prevailing wisdom that may have been the norm before their arrival. Creating a table that fosters the voices of emerging board members is a capacity-deepening investment into the organization's mission-centered legacy.

How might a board cultivate and deepen this mindset? Our experience persuades us it begins as an inside job, with you, a board member. As you take stock of your own satisfaction with your board service moment, in light of the social challenges your board is undertaking, the power move is to nurture a posture of confident humility, that you are sufficient to embody a very serious intention to make a difference through governance. Humility ignites trust. And as humility deepens and trust increases, a board's capacity deepens. This alignment puts a slightly different spin on those logic models that end at the bottom line and on those technicians who cannot see past it to the throbbing purpose for which the board came into existence. This begins from the inside and works its way outward to the social impact intended by its mission.

We invite you and your board to deepen the conversation by making mentionable what's currently "off the table." By *off the table*, we do not mean to suggest anything is untoward or underhanded, as the card-sharking gambler might use the cover of the table's top to intentionally deceive. Again, we think there are plenty of tools (unused, for many boards) already on the table. What the board development conversation seems to lack is a tool to surface what lies *beneath* the table, as it were. When something is off the table, we all know what that means. It is outside the bounds of what we are going to talk about. Out of sight. Out of mind. No boat to rock.

Unconscious.

Therefore, unavailable.

If unavailable, then unmentionable.

If unmentionable, then unmanageable.

Of course, this is how boards get into trouble. This is how "culture eats strategy for breakfast," to quote Peter Drucker. Because we link consciousness with both mentionability and manageability, boards must become conversant with the culture they keep (or which may, in fact, keep them). If a board is going to be blamed or misunderstood unfairly when things go contrary to expectations, should it not invest significant attention to those things for which it indeed wants to be rightfully blamed? We say adopt your values and live into them boldly so that it's absolutely clear which values you intend to be known by, even if it rocks all the boats in the harbor. Many boards excel at this, and we highlight several we hope will encourage you.

However, many board members report that while motivated by the mission, they struggle with their board's culture. And even as boards diversify and bring in underrepresented voices in both the corporate and nonprofit sectors,[4] which are known to improve decision-making, many organizations simply pay lip service. And once an actual person shows up, whose existence differs from the cultural norm of the other board members, that new board member might take the theoretical shine off the board's honest aspirations. Such new members just might use their voice—and it may sound different from any and every other voice in the room that had enjoyed a kind of blind privilege prior to that new member's arrival. They may use the peer authority vested in them by the mission, their membership affirmations and their fidelity to the mission's constituents. When they do, on that day, we will know whether the board, which verbally espoused the culture shift, is equal to their culture change aspirations.

Does your board say things like "We run everything aboveboard here"? Or "We say what we mean, and we mean what we say in meetings." "It is on the agenda, and when we vote, it becomes the law. That's how it gets done." We would like to hope this is how it works. However, we know too many stories of board decisions being made in the parking lot long before the vote was taken at the boardroom table. You *say* that "Robert's Rules of Order" is how you discern and ratify agreements. But the parking lot politicking *is* how your board actually functions, whether it's in the policy manual or not.

We have to talk about this. If a board has deeper conversations, shifting the unmentionable to manageable, that board will set in motion a governance ethos that results in deep impact. And we hope that not only does that impact faithfully serve those to whom the organization has made its mission-based promise, but that its members themselves experience transformation.

When boards practice making the unmentionable mentionable, especially when the matter impacts stakeholders, they gain capacity.

Culture becomes an asset.

Decisions are deepened.

Impact is made and lives are transformed.

Being a culturally conscious board member at this moment requires an intentional look at what's happening on the boardroom table. It requires a look at how the table is set. It invites members to take note of how some of their unspoken parts—humility and trust, undergirded by an ethic of curiosity and welcome—can be enlisted to deepen and accelerate their aspirations to make a lasting impact. This book is our invitation to leverage your board's culture as an asset for social transformation and impact.

PART ONE

Setting the Table for Deeper Impact

In Part One, we describe the predicament in which most boards find themselves. Boards regularly operate at a surface level where service can simply be transactional, rather than transformational. The boardroom table is merely a piece of furniture on which we place our board binders and coffee cups. But what if we have underestimated what's really going on when we convene as a board of governors? What if our best conversational decisions of the past were made on only half the intelligence we needed to decide? Might we have decided differently if all our decision-making assets had been made available, made mentionable? In this part, we take on these questions. We take a closer look at the table, getting beneath the surface of things for a deeper conversation.

1

Board Culture Begins at Home

The woman or man who believes
their mama's bread is the best in the world,
has not traveled very far from home.

GHANAIAN PROVERB

You are a serious person, with limited precious time. We can generate
a list of staccato moralisms for becoming a culturally conscious board
member: Take your seat. Bring all you are to the boardroom. Be conscious of the culture you keep. And these might be instructive. But
when it comes to experienced leaders, edicts and insults seldom make
much of a difference. So, we invite you instead to enter a story.

We invite you to meet Crystal, a new board member. You will get
to know her more intimately as the book unfolds. You will meet Phil,
the board chair. Michael is the treasurer. You might meet a few other
members who may or may not make it to board meetings—you know
how busy board members can be. Each boasts years of board experience and distinctive professional success. Confident, efficient and
ready to contribute, they know how to get things done. In case you
begin to wonder, the people you meet are fictional. What they signify
is real. As we follow each along Crystal's journey, you may find yourself

identifying with their moments of discovery, frustration and even sur-
render—as their board is both made and measured by their inescapable task of culture learning at the boardroom table.

Meet Crystal. She's new to boards, but she's not new to volunteering. Before college, she spent precious hours each week in
the Baker Park neighborhood, working with the food bank and
delivering meals to the elderly. She helped with reading circles
on weekends at the Boys & Girls Club. When her church distributed warm clothing before harsh Buffalo winters, she scavenged
the family's closets for unused coats, gloves and scarves. She
took them to the church's "Pre-Winter Swap Shop" (sometimes
to the teasing chagrin of her older brother, who could be heard
on wintry mornings protesting, "Ma, she did it again! Crystal
gave away my designer puffer this time!"). Crystal cared about
people. Her grandmother's words rang true: "Discomfort is the
price that someone will have to pay on the road to doing the
right thing."

Crystal spent 16 years living in Baker Park before heading off to
college and graduate school. Although she now lives in a thriv-
ing bedroom suburb of Lackawanna, closer to the public health
clinic where she was recently hired as a community nutrition
educator, she still drops into Baker Park most weekends to see
her mom. If the stars all aligned, and her kid sister, Chloe, was
not too heavily medicated by her new drug of choice, she might
get to see Chloe, too. Her mother and her sister were family, not
her mission. She had given up on "fixing" her people years ago.
She watched her mother endure heartache repeatedly as her kid
sister called for bail, called for rent, called for prayer. Crystal's
mother, the sole provider in the home for years, would give
them all, especially the last.

Like everyone at the health clinic, Crystal learned public health administration in the classroom. She was also grateful for streetwise instructors and mentors who allowed her to keep her hands in both the theory and the practice of what she was learning. While in school, Crystal worked as a volunteer night receptionist at a homeless shelter for street kids. She often coordinated with social workers, police and occasionally loved ones calling with "Have you seen a teenage boy, 14, 5′5″, brown hair….He's our son…he's been gone for a few days. We are calling around…." She felt it when those kinds of calls came in. It would take her back to her own chaotic upbringing, remembering how her own mother used similar words with neighbors, when Chloe was really out there, ripping and running. After those volunteer shifts, sometimes all she could muster to keep to her center was a whispered "on earth, as it is in heaven, please."

Theory and practice came together in such a way that she could easily spot economic and social "solutions" that promised results but in the end delivered little.

She watched from the sidelines, as a volunteer in her own city, as programs wasted financial and social capital on superficial responses to seriously complicated situations. She learned, repeatedly, that just because a group's brochure promised to "change the world," there was no guarantee their efforts were doing so. She could list a hundred reasons why such "world changers" seldom did more than record "nickels and noses" for fundraising. She also knew the cynicism of "beneficiaries" who were viewed as dependents and recipients of these safety net programs. The frustration of seeing so much wasted opportunity provoked in her a justice-charged determination to be part of the solution. But the new job she took with the public clinic gave her hope. She was learning loads, meeting all kinds of interesting people and making sense of her city—with adult eyes this time.

It wasn't long before Crystal became curious about Baker Park. What happened to some of the kids she used to read to on Saturday mornings at the Boys & Girls Club? She had always promised that if she ever returned, she was going to give back. And tonight was the beginning of a promise kept. Tonight was her first board meeting.

Cultural Consciousness:
Groups Tend Toward Comfort, Unless…

We use *conscious* in everyday speech. Upon waking in the morning, we might say, "I'm not conscious until I have my first cup of coffee." We would be talking about a fuzzy state in which we were noticing surroundings, being aware and not aware. In an emergency room, we might hear "Is he conscious? Breathing? What are his vital signs?" Consciousness and breathing in this context help a clinician to assess condition. We speak about consciousness in this familiar way, not in any specialized academically mysterious way. Being awake and aware is not the enemy of health, but a vital indicator of it.

But the *"culturally* conscious" part? Admittedly, seldom does the average person modify words with *culturally* in everyday conversation, at least in the way we do with *conscious*. To understand what we mean by *culturally* conscious, picture this scene:

You enter the ballroom of the annual fundraiser, heartily greeting friends and business associates as you make your way to the head table. You are the honored guest, being celebrated for your agency's heroic work. The meal begins—a seamless ballet of unfurling napkins, wordless staff, steaming plates and the polite banter of strangers who will be asked to dig deep for the cause. Mercifully, at least for the introverts, a master of ceremonies takes the stage. As chairs turn and coffee cups are topped off, she invites you to the podium. You start up the stairs. She slows as she hands over the microphone, whispering, "You've got spinach in your teeth."

In that exact instant you realize a full-blown standing ovation has begun and *every* eye is trained on you. No time for a mirror. You step to the podium. Your lips begin to part but, *Spinach!*—your internal 911 dispatcher hits the alert button. Internal red lights flash and sirens blare. Like a once-sleeping firefighter stepping into bedside-ready boots, your body's stress control system goes to work: muscles tense, breath deepens, hands grip podium, prefrontal cortex searches for just the right next-step script. This all unfolds in less time than it takes to say "Good evening, friends." You painstakingly enunciate the first words on your index cards. You stammer and hesitate as your body strategizes with its strapped resources to figure out how it is going to smile and not smile while speaking for the next 25 minutes. You are *conscious*.

Ever had a spinach-in-the-teeth day like this? We have—too many times to count. *That's* consciousness. It is the mental attention or concentration we exert. So what's the *culture* part of the "culturally conscious board"? And what does that have to do with the spinach-grinning speaker in the scene above? Culture is your way of being and doing life together. It is the symbols, the unspoken codes of conduct, as well as the written ones. Culture is the way, our way, the right way. No board needs a spinach-in-the-teeth day through their way of doing life together. The threat of cancel-culture-like reactions can seriously compound the ethical calculations boards make when deliberating. No board needs the embarrassment that comes with collectively missing what hides in plain sight. Quite the opposite, we wish every board would or could be spared this, but decisions matter.

We state a basic assumption in the Introduction—boards make

decisions. As a board member, you stand with your organization in the gap between the *world as it is* and the *world as it can be* if your mission succeeds. In other words, the best of board work results in transformation. For this reason, *a culturally conscious board explicitly considers culture—that of the board, its stakeholders and the wider society in which it serves—as a shaping influence in its deliberations toward intended impact. It intentionally seeks to be aware of its own culture, while also acknowledging its own cultural blindfolds.* To be culturally conscious is fundamental to a board's integrity. It is fundamental to its fiduciary purpose of mission fulfillment.

We make a secondary assumption. You would prefer to make decisions in a diligent, generous and circumspect manner. You want to work smarter, not harder. For this reason, when board members receive their board meeting package late, or with just a few hours to review complicated documents due for a vote that same day, that simple practice impacts the decision quality of that team. If your board consists of 10 members and 4 or 5 are consistently absent, those behaviors impact the decision outcomes of that board. If your board provides nurses abroad but does not have nurse insights represented at the boardroom table, then the impact of your decisions is affected during a crisis because it lacks integrity.

No board would stomach even the hint of an allegation that it lacked integrity in its decision-making. Assuming integrity is related only to honesty, a board so accused would begin to gladly invite accountability and transparency. "Come, look through all our books, our minutes, our conflict-of-interest agreements—look everywhere and you will find no evidence of wrongdoing, no breach of integrity," your board would protest. And rightfully so, if integrity pertained only to honesty. But *integrity* has a wider semantic range, and this range is important to the work we do in defining culture's role in board decision-making. Integrity also means *completeness, coherence* and *wholeness.* A brand-new tire with a pinhole lacks a kind of integrity that is not theoretical. We know the practical implications. Knowing whether the tires you rely on have small holes in them or not is a case of whether you are conscious of the tire's integrity or not.

We think of *consciousness* as a *heightened focus provoked by our surroundings and experiences, enabling us to predict and participate with integrity in the world around us.* It may be involuntary and passive in response to a stimulus, such as smelling coffee upon waking. Or it might be the kind of mental exertion we use if typing a text while running hurriedly through an airport to catch a soon-departing flight. In this sense, consciousness means paying attention—it exerts focus so as to not miss things, to capture everything essential, to keep everything that pertains together. A decision has integrity only if all the factors that matter to its success are duly considered.

When decisions are made on behalf of others, naturally, their definition of success overrides yours. Catching yourself in the act of presumption is extremely difficult when acting alone. However, no mission exists in a social vacuum. Every mission is suspended in a web of stakeholder relationships. If you invite these connections into your capacity-deepening process, you will not only evade the ethnocentric know-it-all spirituality that made uncomfortable classics out of Eugene Burdick and William J. Lederer's *The Ugly American,* Chinua Achebe's *Things Fall Apart* or Barbara Kingsolver's *Poisonwood Bible,* but you will position yourself and your organization for a dialogue between equals out of which sustainability, reciprocity and lasting impact may emerge.

The culturally conscious board decides in consultation with its stakeholders, especially those with the smallest amount of power to exert their own will and resources. It is conscious of the role that culture—the cohesion system of any membership group—plays in the survival and sustainability of that group. Culture is active in at least three senses in this working definition. In this description of consciousness, culture is a provocateur of *why* a matter may get heightened focus, perhaps explaining how different groups might have differing lenses and scales for what *ought* to provoke attention and participation. Culture plays a sense-making role enabling or disenabling *how* we interface with the world, through construction, conduct and communication, those things we make, how we act and with whom. Culture is the internally imposed arbiter between *what* we say we are doing and what we are actually doing.

A culturally conscious board is interested in how culture shapes the services it delivers and how its governance meets the cultural requirements of various stakeholders in its fulfillment process. When cultural difference calls for a culture shift to better ensure that mission intent is kept, the culturally conscious board makes that shift. The culturally conscious board revises its assumptions, processes, policies and procedures as it learns more and more about the implications of its policy reach with the people who care about the organization's ability to act with integrity and partnership with them. Such a board, upon learning that a cultural difference has emerged that impacts its ability to serve, initiates consultation by explicitly asking for help from its own members to access (and assess!) their own experience with that difference, or it widens its consultation circle to include coaches and cultural mentors.

Your board is subject to the social laws that shape all working groups. Like natural laws, when you perceive them, respect them or even work with them, these laws reward. Disregard these physical laws, in some cases for even an instant, and the natural world claps back quite insistently and unforgivingly in assigning consequences, some of which may be irreversible. Pull together a chair, treasurer and secretary and a charter and bylaws, then register and pay fees with your secretary of state, and boom, you have a board, an organization—on paper. Beyond this foundational legal structuring phase, what a board becomes will follow the patterns of what most all groups become, a comfort zone. That is what we do as humans. Norms are good. But norms also have a way of rocking us to sleep, dulling us into spectators, requiring little of our critical faculties. Culture is happy to provide a bed. It is likely to resemble your boardroom table.

You Have a Culture...You Have Manners

While the principles of *The Culturally Conscious Board: Setting the Boardroom Table for Impact* may apply to any board, it is our intention to address those on whom many of us around the planet have staked some of our deepest humanitarian hopes—the *transformation sector.* We are burdened most for you. We think you and your boards matter.

And so we sat down at a table together and raised some questions: Why are we—Jennifer and Russell—writing this? A conversation unfolded about our experiences in diverse decision-making settings and how these shaped the roads we took and did not take. We recounted the culturally rich family legacies shaping our identities, the gritty and foolhardy service projects, the prejudices that confused and humiliated us in some of the unlikeliest of places on Earth. We asked, What do we have to give, to whom? On whose behalf do we write? We noticed common lessons entrusted to us by thousands who may never set foot out of their cities and villages, but whose faces and predicaments we pledged to remember in solidarity. We took time to listen to each other's stories.

As we hinted in the Preface, our roots are in community development and capacity building, at home and abroad. We have been nonprofit entrepreneurs multiple times over. Having both enjoyed higher education careers as leadership educators, we continue to encourage and be inspired by the social impact efforts of thousands of leaders we were privileged to serve. We have started, served, consulted and coached boards. Both career adult educators of leadership, we happened upon a shared assumption and sobered realization about how leaders are formed and fortified: *Leaders are welcomed to the table. But how many are not yet invited, whose voices are needed to better serve the missions that transform communities?*

Think about your own leadership journey. Think about how you were formed, validated and told "you belong at the leadership table." Do you remember someone inviting you, telling you, in so many words, that you just might have what it takes to be a leader? Was it at a Sunday afternoon dinner, when your grandpa said, "I'd like you to have something I've saved for you—it's my old briefcase…you'll need it someday"? Did a high school coach call you over during practice and say, "Watch your temper. These kids look up to you. You keep losing it, you'll lose their respect and we all lose"? That was a call to take your seat. And if you are going to be at the leadership table, where decisions are made, your mindset matters.

Cultural Home: How Culture Forms

Russ was a professor for a significant season of his life. In a course called Leadership in a Multicultural Society, he required learners to write a "my cultural journey" paper, a project that allowed each to revisit critical cross-cultural turning points in their cultural identity development. One paper sticks out in his mind. It's the story of Kevin. His opening line is still arresting to this day: "I don't have a culture. I guess American is my culture. I'm just a white guy from Kansas. I wish I had a culture."[5] Russ recalls hot tears of compassion involuntarily brimming his eyelids as he absorbed these vulnerable words.

Just was pregnant with street-level implications for the people this leader would one day serve. Can you imagine an intercultural encounter—usually requiring at least two cultures to tango—in which only one of the parties is conscious of having a culture, only one is aware they have and have always had a cultural identity? Of course, as a person of color, Russ is quite cognizant of being the recipient of a cultural story. By *recipient* he means recipient of a gift or an invitation. With all the social mirrors, how could someone miss the gift of their own cultural identity?

Being born into a Black family in America, at a time when his own civil rights were not protected by law, he would know the contours of what W. E. B. Dubois meant by every Black man, at some time in his life, will have to reckon with the crisis of being Black.[6] For Russ, it was not a matter of whether he had a cultural story, but what this consciousness required of him.

Receiving our social location, in all its richness and complexity, is akin to receiving any gift. One is grateful. One stewards and does not squander. One is not too proud, after all it was received. One permits no acts of shame from others, after all it was a gift. If you ask Russ where this generous perspective comes from, he will smile, thinking fondly of his late father, Ralph, a tall, handsome U.S. Marine Corps master sergeant who exuded a calm, nurturing presence at home and a serious bent to fidelity and duty to society. He will share tender stories of his mid-90s mother, Mildred, a dynamite 4'11" West Virginia coal miner's daughter, whose watchwords were *self-respect, self-sufficiency* and *self-giving* to others. As a military family, they lived in a lot of places, traveled lots. She would marshal them before a road trip with "Now each of you pack and carry your own bags." She insisted each of her children "stand up tall, stand up for what's right and stand up for those who can't do so themselves." His parents modeled an appreciation for their own story and for that of others on equal terms. More importantly, they emphasized the kind of person each child was obliged to become. To add an urgency to integrity-keeping, his dad would remind them: "It's later than you think."

Russ became a conscious steward of his ethnicity and cultural identity. When at varied leadership tables, he expects himself and others to be cognizant and conversant in their own cultural story as stewards, neither too proud nor ever ashamed. He commends this posture of grateful humility as foundational to a culturally conscious leader and board. From this starting place, we not only claim our seats, but we enroll in a culture learning journey so we know what to do with them once there.

Cultural Superiority: We All Begin in a Cultural Home

On the back stairs of the Jukanovich house are family photographs that go back five generations on each side, with each frame telling a different story. There's one of the great-great-grandfather, a Polish immigrant, who was shot in the back and killed during a mining strike known as the Hazleton Massacre; the great-grandmother from Paris who gave away her inheritance to marry a WWI soldier who was actually a philandering eccentric inventor; the grandmother who performed an opera recital in Carnegie Hall once but never fully realized her dreams; the Montenegrin immigrant who returned to his homeland to fight against the armies of Austria-Hungary; the German great-grandfather who ruled his domain with an iron fist; the mother inflicted with polio at the age of seventeen—story after story.

Jennifer's daughter asked her once why they even have these photos on display if there are so many sad stories. Pointing to the last few and more recent photographs, Jennifer shared, in this teachable moment: "The successes and the challenges have formed our family over generations. They make us, for good and bad, who we are. And now, we have the chance to write a new story." You see, the Jukanovich children, today, represent the rest of the family story. Their own birth cultures, through adoption from their homelands of China and Rwanda, beautify and deepen the story, through both heartache and hope. Yet, when forming their new family, Dano and Jennifer were faced with questions from a few relatives: "Why not try other methods first before adoption?" "So, there'll be a yellow daughter?" "Africa?! That means he'll be black? What's wrong with kids from here?" Blood mattered. And while blood is red, the color of skin mattered more to a few. Fortunately, most of the family was welcoming, but words of a few matter and hurt.

We all have a story, and applying the standard of one's cultural group as the choice that's superior to those of others is very common and natural. It's often called ethnocentrism, a preference for "your mama's bread" over that of other membership groups. When it is unmentionable, when it's off the table, then that biased preference can find its way into a dozen seemingly unrelated expressions or microaggressions, such as a raised eyebrow at a colleague's idea, a "no" vote in which you insist on things being done your way or the highway. At least until that guest or stranger becomes the one whose way differs from yours.

Cultural Inferiority: Mistakenly Leaving Home Behind

If ethnocentrism distorts our relationships by its over-identification with self, its opposite is just as destructive. Consider the Jukanovich family wall again. If in seeking to honor her children's cultures, Jennifer removes all references to the European ancestry that shapes her, seeking to leave it behind, she is not being true to her cultural formation. In fact, to remove those references is to nurture fiction. In Russ's recollection of a student who had abdicated the gift of cultural identity, he stewards his comparative experience with cultural identity as an empathic bridge. Leveraging his own cultural consciousness as a warrant to speak up (a consciousness wrought by keeping a grounded dignity amid society's fickle political interest games with his ethnic and racial demographic standing), he can relate to the learner's self-limiting belief—as a receiver of his social membership, and not from the power position that the learner *should* think otherwise, simply because of his authority as a professor.

Just as Jennifer encouraged her daughter, Russ fostered curiosity in a fellow learner as to whether cultural vacancy is even possible. Being culturally neutral is a convenient cop-out tactic that leaves well-defended comfort zones unperturbed. It leaves relevant participants off the guest list for the corporate work party that has to build and nurture a culture in which we all can flourish. Each is part of a story, and stories touch, conflict, converge and move on. But no one is a cultural bystander. Everyone has a cultural home.

So the boardroom table, a table set in particular cultural spaces with members hailing each from their own rich cultural homes, can become what Romanita Hairston calls "an island of sanctuary" for you, *and* maybe you alone if none on your board will go with you, *to experiment with the beauty, dignity and responsibility that comes with stewarding a seat at a boardroom table.*

Cultural Humility: A Learning Path for Board Members

While we direct our attention to *boards* in *The Culturally Conscious Board*, we invite you to test our assumptions with other deliberative bodies you may be a part of, such as councils, committees and working groups. It is extremely difficult to come into consciousness in isolation. There is that moment of truth all humans experience when we receive the gift of seeing ourselves as others might see us. We realize not only do we have bread we prefer, our mama's bread, but we see *they* have mamas and breads they love too. And we can both stand with ourselves fully clothed in our rich cultural wardrobe, and also simultaneously appreciate that they, too, are richly garbed in their cultural finest.

In the thickness of socially constructed barriers that frustrate and divide, a narrowing occurs where each, equal in the dignity of their shared humanity, experiences a little more room. Empathy renders a service: we uphold appreciative mirrors for one another. In humility, we are conscious of our own vulnerability to spinach-grin moments. We cultivate tables safe enough to say to each other, "Hey, you might want to take a glance in the mirror before getting up on stage."

The social impact sector is run through with idealistic change agents of every stripe, but unless some things get said, some decisions will be processed as sorely anemic. Many rely on you and your vision of a better world. You must get this, or *who else* will? So, we want to help. We want to encourage your important work as agents of transformation at the boardroom table. So, whether you:

are a fumbling, eagle-eyed start-up,

said yes but are unsure where to start,

will ever get the chance to attend a board training event,

are a seasoned board member suddenly in the hot seat,

wonder if you are doing any good by sitting in late-night meetings, bickering over a dollar,

are tired of constantly being the guest in a story that doesn't appreciate yours,

we say, this book is written for you.

THE TAKE-HOME BOX

The Take-Home Boxes at the ends of the first five chapters acknowledge that although we seek to set a table at which board members can get beyond the surface and into the heart of the matter in their decision-making, some of the work is yours and yours alone. The Take-Home Boxes offer a few questions that invite you to think more deeply about your boardroom culture.

What are some of your cultural identity turning points?

- Can you share a time you began to see yourself as you were seen by others, especially those whose cultural backgrounds differed from your own?

- Can you detect cultural superiority or inferiority in yourself? Others? How?

- Can you relate to the temptation to wish for a "culturally neutral" identity? How does your answer impact your ability to detect your board's cultural tendencies?

- Can you recall when you received a gift that arose from the cultural heritage of others that was different from your own?

2

Table Culture

My wish, my continuing passion, would be not to point the finger in judgment, but to part a curtain, that invisible shadow that falls between people, the veil of indifference to each other's presence, each other's wonder, each other's human plight.

EUDORA WELTY[7]

Crystal shook herself from her memories, just as Phil, the board chair, loudly cracked a gavel on a wooden block, precisely at 7:00 p.m. sharp!

"All rise! I now call the board to order. We will begin tonight as we always do, by reciting the Pledge of Allegiance." The gavel clacked on its wooden base three times, each amplifying the nerve-rattling effect of the other in the echoey commercial kitchen.

They sat at a table someone had pulled out. This table had its own storage room when they were not gathered. It was a (too) small, four-by-seven-foot, 19th-century antique wooden table that once belonged to Phil's great-grandfather. Phil came from a farming family in upstate New York, and when he became founding chair, he insisted that City Farm accept the table as a gift, "from one farmer to another." It was beautiful—carved on four sides, with distinctively fashioned lion heads, bearing open jaws and teeth. Two drawers flanked each side, where notepads, old agendas, pens and a few candy wrappers could always be found.

All the board members began to shuffle their chairs and amble to their feet; scratching and clawing sounds echoed from the hard- wood floors of the old kitchen. Crystal attempted to make small talk as they took their positions, but there wasn't time. Phil, a commercial real estate agent and now a recent retiree from the New York National Guard, bellowed with a well-practiced emo- tional cadence that gave everyone time to speak with one voice: "I pledge allegiance, to the flag." A chorus of stalwart baritone voices—Crystal was the only soprano board member present tonight—issued forth from the small room, echoing down the hallway of the old Boys & Girls Club turned kitchen.

Though Crystal stood and mouthed the words, the pledge faded into the background as her mind was seized with sev- eral questions at once: Will they start these with that hammer every time? Had she heard of a board meeting starting with the Pledge of Allegiance? Wasn't there another woman on the board, Jemma? Surely, she thought, someone will tell me what I am supposed to do. With this beginning and this many questions in so few minutes, she felt a lump in her throat. She swallowed. The reality of what it might mean to be on *this* board was coming home. There were rules in place of which she knew little. Who did she think she was, joining this board—at least, if this is how the first few minutes of her first-ever board meeting started out.

"And to the Republic for which it stands," the pledge contin- ued to go by her. Crystal was very patriotic, having grown up hearing the stories of sacrifice from her grandfather in WWII.

> But something felt *off*. "What have I gotten myself into?" she
> nervously pondered.

A Boardroom Is Never Empty

Given the table's propensity to evoke a disposition of awareness (or as
we will argue later, consciousness), we offer the table here as a metaphor. And we assert up front: most of what you need to be "culturally
conscious" you already internalize. The boardroom table itself forms
the mental model that boards need to rest upon to generate a more
conscious workplace for fiduciary service. The table is an ancient player
in the minds of people serious about getting things done the right way.

A boardroom is never "empty."

At the center of the typical boardroom, *a table* is its crowning feature. It is the silent centerpiece upon which we lay our papers, set our
cups, write our notes—at times pound our fists or want to bang our
heads. The table is a supporting cast member in every boardroom
drama. It permits and constrains. It has rules. The table undergirds
and formalizes every decision hammered out upon its surface.

Even if the members of the board are at their homes, fast asleep,
the room's décor continues to speak. The "rules of order" remain internally lodged and ready to resume their choreographing persistence.
The record of minutes and agendas attests to priorities solemnized in
permanent records. Portraits of "those who have gone before us" stare
down upon proceedings in some boardrooms, with the stern and im-
passive countenances of judges, warning those who follow not to stray
from *the way* handed down.

A boardroom is *never* empty.

A table abides there.

From a cultural perspective, *the table* is never neutral. It beckons.

There is a sense that the table can insist on truth, visibility and solemnity like few cultural artifacts can. "I'll just put all my cards on the table." "So, now that's off the table, we can decide." "He turned the tables on me and I was trapped." "Let's table that until we get more clarity." "They've earned a seat at the table." "He was paying them, under the table."

The table has solidity. We are *at* the table. Things are *on* the table or *off* the table. The table holds—"Let's table that until...." The table does not tolerate—"You may not, not at *this* table." The table extends—"There will always be room at our table for...."

Every Table Has Its Rules

What do *manners* and *boardrooms* have to do with each other? How do "boardroom manners" relate to the boardroom as a workplace? The question is an important one.

You have heard people say something like this, perhaps when you were growing up:

"Elbows off the table, son."

"Sit up straight, please."

"Please don't talk with your mouth full."

"Let us bow our heads and give thanks."

We could go on, but we think you get the point: tables have their rules that echo over thousands of tables every day, in all kinds of languages. Although known the world over as easygoing or informal in their manners, most Americans can in fact be exacting when it comes to what's in and out when it comes to table time. But to be clear, Americans are not odd in this.

Etiquette experts tell us *every* culture has its own rules of engagement, its customs and courtesies when it comes to gathering at tables for food, trade or decisions. In Thailand, a child might hear "Don't leave the table until you've had three cups of tea." In Korea, a well-mannered child knows "a table is not a place for talking, but for eating." In Russia, toasts are made in order—first by the host for the guest, then the guest for the host, followed by a toast for the women and always with a glass of vodka on the table before each new round. In Ethiopia, it is expected that one dips the *injera* into shared platters of curry and stew. In Britain, it's "Make no noise with your spoon while stirring the tea—and do *not* leave the spoon standing in the cup!" Such "dos and don'ts" may hearken back to our own family gatherings or the first time we traveled to a country with different table manners than our own family's rules. The bottom line: we have an uncanny ability to check ourselves, to get with the program that tables require of us.

What we propose is a critical reflection that allows boards to engage in a series of conversations at their tables that are right for the cultural moment in which we find ourselves. We evoke "table manners" as the mental organizing model to assist with this. Every culture has manners that are observed when groups gather for various purposes. Sometimes elaborate formal protocols can shape, if not prescribe, every fine detail of an event right down to who sits next to whom or the order and space between forks, knives and spoons. At other times, our impulse for protocol appears less formal, less elaborate, showing itself in invitations as "Dress Code: Business Casual" or "Bring your own brown bag…we'll be working through lunch."

These nudges for our participation—customs, conduct and even clothing—are so ordinary, so normal that we are hard-pressed to give them much thought. Of course, that is the nature of culture—it serves as the set of customs and behaviors we follow within our various groups, helping us maintain harmony, strengthen togetherness and set boundaries. This holds true on a larger scale, where cultures represent entire nations, languages and politically bordered regions. It also applies to smaller groups such as communities and families. In any cultural context, both the broader nationwide culture and the specific localized cultures play a role, even when dealing with varying degrees of diversity and cultural differences.

Every board has a culture. It is your way of being and doing life together. It is the symbols, the unspoken codes of conduct, as well as the written ones. It is easy to talk about those board rituals that are practiced regularly out in the open, even by agreement. In many cases, these become its policies and practices. Oftentimes, board culture is the result of a group having resolved yesteryear's stabilize-or-sustain problems for itself. The values that would first react to external influence or threats can either accelerate or decelerate your success. These are the same values and attitudes that are currently shaping the decision-making framework of your board and its deliberations. And since it—the stabilize-or-sustain problem—has been solved, it is too easy to put off thinking deeply about these. Over time, they become unmentionable or simply taken for granted. They keep the structures of our lives afloat, moving forward and making sense.

Most boards, if asked about this, might refute this and say, "We do nothing except by explicit agreement" or "On our board, we invite folks to mean what they say and say what they mean." To borrow a term from personal computing, this is the "WYSIWYG" view of board culture—"What you see is what you get." And most boards we know don't intentionally seek to have policies and practices as mechanisms by which needed voices might be silenced.

It has been our experience that it is seldom just the policies and practices—the *mentionable*—that cause the most problems. It's rather the *unmentionable* aspects of unconscious culture that strengthen and weaken in their influence as long as they remain unnamed. Our task is to point out that you already have a set of boardroom manners you strictly follow. The question we raise is whether these help or hinder your decision-making work. Wouldn't you want to know where denial or negligence has caused culture to be a liability?

THE TAKE-HOME BOX

- How would you describe your board's rules of engagement, its customs and courtesies when it comes to gathering at the boardroom table?

- What are two policies or practices that shape how you make decisions?

- How were you welcomed as a newcomer to the board? What part of your orientation helped you understand the undergirding values of the board and the organization?

- If you are on more than one board, how do these values compare to or contradict one another?

3

On and Off the Table

It always disturbed me how many biographers never gave their subjects a chance to eat. You can tell a lot about people by how they eat, what they eat, and what kind of table manners they have.

DAVID MCCULLOUGH[8]

Crystal knew volunteering. She knew Baker Park (at least she did when she was a kid growing up there). But the growing sensation in the pit of her stomach after her first board meeting left her with the question, What did it mean to be on a *board*?

She kept reminding herself to give herself some grace. This was her first tentative step into an unfamiliar world, one with rituals, customs and speech different from her workplace meetings, book club and pickup basketball league. Luckily, tonight she realized she knew at least one other person in the room—Sierra. During her literacy work, she used to read to Sierra and other kids. And now Sierra was the executive director of City Farm, a nonprofit that literally and figuratively arose from the ashes when the Boys & Girls Club burned down almost 10 years ago. Sierra, with the help of a wide-ranging network of funders, restaurants and community garden projects, had found a new use for the once-burned-out Boys & Girls Club building. Until Sierra got involved after completing her MBA, that building was that place you did not go to after dark, unless you were looking for trouble, drugs or prostitutes.

Sierra was four years into rewriting the building's story. She and many Baker Park residents had petitioned the city of Lackawanna to sell the building to a new project she called City Farm. City Farm would not be a nonprofit agency there "to help the poor," she argued in her petition, but would rather partner with the community's people and assets to furnish a safe learning environment in which residents could incubate their own businesses, learn supporting skills from mentors and reshape the generational economic prospects for this part of the city. City Farm's flagship program was Waste Not, Want Not, a food-farm-family food recovery project. It brought together a network of restaurants and grocery stores to recapture their food surplus. It developed a patchwork of community and immigrant gardens that supplied fresh vegetables and fruits to source the City Farm Kitchen. "The Kitchen" supplied ready-to-travel hot, nutritious meals to several partner assisted-living homes, homeless shelters and an elementary school nearby. City Farm even had a composting business, run by a couple of the guys who had lived at the shelter. They sold their compost to a gardening wholesaler in Buffalo. City Farm's tag line read "Transform the soil—seeds will take it from there."

Sierra was putting her MBA to work and in so doing had put 140 immigrants, refugees and a few single moms to work. The mentored job-creation model was the engine of City Farm. The food recapture process was a daily task involving food handling and cooking classes, kitchen supply and food service management, a food and beverage industry marketing course and basic computing skills. Several new immigrants got help with English as a second language from senior Kitchen buddies. City Farm was growing. It had received a bump in visibility last year when the mayor's office selected it for one of its City Heroes awards. An influx of new donors, foundations and media attention positioned City Farm for expansion of its current facility. The City of Buffalo had also called, suggesting real interest in helping City Farm establish a new site in Buffalo.

Crystal had no idea of all that had been happening with Sierra until she had gone to a fundraising event the year before. She could hardly believe that her "Lil Sierra" was more than all grown up—she was an emerging civic and economic development force for good in the neighborhood where they both grew up. Crystal was inspired and wanted to help wherever Sierra thought it best. Sierra asked if Crystal would consider joining the board. With all the programs, attention and new possibilities, Sierra needed a few new teammates in whom she could confide and trust. On that invitation alone, Crystal was *in*.

So, while Crystal was not a stranger to Baker Park and her old friend from the neighborhood, she had to admit she didn't really know what she had committed to as a board member.

Assets and Liabilities

Two board members joined a nonprofit board at the same time. A friend of ours is one of them. And she is the board's first woman of color. During her first meeting, she spoke confidently as an attorney to a point of law. Her point, however, spoiled the executive director's plan. The other first-timer, taking the pulse of furtive glances between a few antsy members, took a "watch first, speak later" tactic. Word got back to our friend that the executive director fumed about this in front of his staff: "How dare she? Doesn't she know you aren't supposed to

speak at your first board meeting? You are supposed to listen and ob
serve. Why can't she be like *him*!?" Ambiguous at best: she would be
more acceptable in silence, divining unwritten norms, becoming a
man? Pejorative at its worst: was the executive director talking about
racialized preferences, out loud? Courageous, a team member asked,
"Were these rules clear to new members? Isn't that why you courted
her, for her expertise?" Two new board members. Two different experiences; both evaluated on unspoken rules.

Only those who are witnesses to what happens at your table can
understand the role culture *is* playing in the outcomes of your work.
Usually, it is an asset or a liability. It is also likely your board has a
mixture of both. Most boards would answer honestly that the answer
depends. It depends on who you ask. It depends on whether they are
longtimers or newcomers (my, don't they *both* miss a lot). It depends
on the agenda. Sometimes we aren't even aware until someone makes
a motion to change something.

Table Culture: The Culture Shift

It is out of our profound respect for you and the ripple effect of what
you do as a board member that we ask, What difference would be made
in the world if a board were to sit down and have an honest conversation about their *culture*?

There are plenty of boards whose table culture looks a lot like a
formal legal proceeding or a parliamentary committee meeting. The
job around that table is to arrive *on time*, be congenial (but it is *not
required that* you become friends before *joining*), *consent* to an *agenda*,
approve minutes, *listen* to reports, *stick* to the agenda, keep comments
brief and on point, have *read* (or appear to have read) *all* the materials
before the meeting, *contribute* something every time (*analytic precision*
is welcome, but *don't rock the boat*), signify your *vote* when the question
is called—until that moment when everyone good-naturedly laughs

when the *board chair* finally asks, "*Do I hear a movement to adjourn?*" at which point there are so many chairs scraping floors that the "Second" is drowned out and conversations in the parking lot ensue until the board meets to *do it all over again* next month. The *same people* (unless they are *absent*—then they are *those other same people who are absent*), the *same way*.

If your board meeting runs similar to the one we just described, then you have not only well-established boardroom manners, but also manners that are wrapped in specific cultural clothing that have been passed down. Major Henry Martyn Robert was a U.S. Army engineer. While volunteering at a San Francisco church in the early 1900s, one that reflected the many different nationalities of the Bay Area at the time, he became baffled by their tumultuous meetings. Using as a model the U.S. Congress's parliamentary procedures (which themselves are modeled on early Presbyterian session, or board, meetings), Robert sketched out a little field guide to help his church ensure every voice received a fair chance to be heard, in an orderly, inclusive fashion. The book, *Pocket Manual of Rules of Order for Deliberative Assemblies*, was eventually dubbed "Robert's Rules of Order" as it grew in popularity. It continues in print today; it was the original "board book of manners."

This approach to collaborative decision-making has been around for a long, long time. You can even say it has been passed down as *the* way a board meeting is *supposed* to run. Do a Google search or ask ChatGPT "I'm a new board member, what should I expect?" and we are pretty sure it will describe your *role*—wait, there goes that ritual language again—in a manner that would help you fit right in with the parliamentary boardroom table we have described above.

Do not get us wrong. There is nothing wrong with rituals. They work. But being more pointed: What *comes to mind* when the word *ritual* is mentioned? What images come to mind? Does your mind go to religious ceremonies, weddings, burials, holiday decorating, bowing or

FIGURE 3.1 Conscious Culture

shaking hands, or greetings that can be thoughtlessly answered with "I'm fine" (even if we are not)? This is the practical stuff of culture.

On such a parliamentary board, whatever is on the table are the rituals. Good board meetings and good board members *stick* to the agenda. The agenda governs the action. The sum total of a board's work is constrained by the process by which items get on and off the agenda. Based on the principle that in a deliberative body, every voice deserves a chance to speak and be heard, parliamentary procedures offer a way to facilitate that. It is laborious and clunky at times, but going by the book has been the way to go for a long time and in a lot of places, mostly as an export of colonial European nations. In parliamentary mode, *that which is on the table is the agenda and that which is on the agenda is on the table.* There is nothing else to see here.

Based on our lived experience with governance teams, there is a *lot* more to see. And not only see, but hear, feel and express. People who join boards deserve appreciation for their agreement to serve the greater good through their service as trustees. But if you cannot

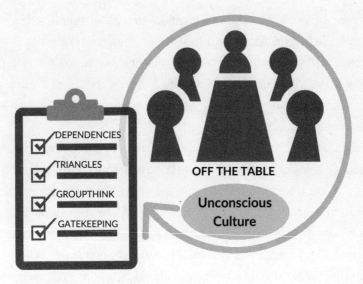

FIGURE 3.2 Unconscious Culture

make your board's culture mentionable (or your own received cultural identity, for that matter), most likely it is doing just as it is specifically designed to do—keep things *out of mind*. Culture does not like to be the news. It deals in artifacts, customs and rituals. Take a glance at the italicized words at the beginning of this section; these speak to a kind of parliamentary decision-making culture, at least the visible and tangible dimension. This is culture "on the table." Social scientists call it "conscious culture," those observable parts we experience with our five senses. But that is only half the story (see Figure 3.1).

The other half of the story is called "unconscious culture." The undergirding principles and practices governing everything, from who gets the inside jokes to why the rules appear to get unevenly applied, are the domain that is usually out of sight and out of mind. This is how the board, or any membership group actually, operates. Unseen and perhaps thought to be "immaterial," this makes up the other part of the story and lies hidden under the table (see Figure 3.2).

Boards operate at half capacity when only at the transactional level that conscious culture tends to provide—agendas, minutes, budgets and strategies, for example. All first-order changes take place at this conscious surface level. A first-order change when you're trying to quit smoking, for example, is throwing away cigarettes and ash trays or wearing a nicotine patch. All visible and material. But is that how people stop smoking?

Boards operate at deep capacity governance, driven by a view of integrity that includes all that is conscious (mentionable) and unconscious (unmentionable). In the smoking example, when unconscious beliefs, emotional states, living patterns and relationships change, many report a "miraculous" reduction in the desire or even taste for cigarettes. We understand this at the habit-change level. When this unconscious level is made mentionable and habits are changed, then all that is conscious can become subject to discussion, critique and debate. Figure 4.1 in the next chapter shows how even a few of these, like hidden agendas, absenteeism, scarcity mentality and even waste, cause tears in a board's decision-making process, affecting policies and ultimately impact.

Table culture is not neutral and can affect the organization. Given the propensity to create echo chambers that reduce the quality and reach of decisions, it is in the best interests of boards to adopt culture-shifting practices that widen their view of their task. Generating culture shifts on your board will require working both sides of the table, making the unnamed and unmanaged a working part of the governance oversight systems of your board. Culture speaks for itself in what we deal with and do not deal with. The consciousness-raising question we raise here is whether it speaks for you? As we'll discover in the next chapter, doing this hard work requires deep trust.

THE TAKE-HOME BOX

- Using the table-as-culture metaphor in this chapter, list observable practices and artifacts a newcomer might experience if they visited your boardroom table. What's "off the table," not observable but palpable and influential, but undiscussed or even named?

- Think about the next board meeting. How might your board welcome a newcomer differently as a result of this reading?

- Reflect on a crisis your board has faced. How were decisions made during that time? Did your board culture help in the crisis? Did it hinder? Does your board have a conscious, explicit, agreed-upon crisis communication plan? Have the newcomers been oriented into this plan so that everyone knows what to do when the time comes?

- Look over your last strategic plan. What did your board "wish for"? What did your board fund? How does the strategic plan reflect assumptions, intentions and investments for "on the table" priorities? How did your "off the table" cultural influences participate in the shaping of the strategy, its priorities and measures?

- What values might a newcomer most detect after reviewing your minutes, agendas, budgets, policy manuals, performance evaluations and strategies?

PART TWO

The Culturally
Conscious Mindset

In Part Two we look at the board from an inside-out view. As goes the board, so goes the organization—one decision at a time. If this is so, then we have some work to do, within and without. For mission-centered people and board teams, we expect the decision to join a board is for the purpose of transformation. In this part of the book, we look at how the empowering mindset of cultural humility—something anthropologists and interculturalists have known and sought to foster since these disciplines took root a century ago—engenders trust and impact. Board service can benefit from these hard-won social practices and mindsets.

4

Trustee Begins with Trust

*Withholding your true self puts a cap on trust
and on your ability to lead.*

FRANCES X. FREI AND ANNE MORRISS[9]

As the gavel cracked for the next agenda item, Crystal straightened her pressed navy jacket, arranged the notebook in front of her and prepared to be introduced.

Phil, the board chair, began, "Thank you everyone for being here. We have a lot of important items to discuss today. I realize you just received the agenda items a few minutes before the meeting, but City Farm has been doing great in the news and Sierra is doing a decent job, so there shouldn't be any issues.

"I'm also glad we have a new board member here with us. Crystal, welcome." Crystal shifted in her chair, gazed confidently at the other members and prepared to respond with why she was excited to be there. Opening her mouth, she began to smile into her first words of gratitude to the committee. It soon became clear to Crystal that Phil had only exhaled and meant to charge on through the agenda, as written. He did.

Crystal stared into the cracks of the antique table, which at first she hadn't noticed but now felt like a metaphor for the gap she felt. "It's not a big deal," she told herself. "I'm sure there will be other times for connecting with the other members. I'm sure they have a plan for that afterward—maybe?"

This happened sometimes. She knew this feeling from other times when she was a newbie. She liked being an introvert. Being naturally quiet, she was also naturally observant, curious and provoked to deep thought about what was unfolding in the social space before her. What, then, was making her feel unsure, even in her own head? She was becoming aware that this would not be the kind of volunteer gig where she could take a mental vacation from what she did all day. This would require her to practice the same kind of vigilance and culture-switching that worked in her profession as a clinical nutritionist.

She could do this. She knew she could. She stared down at her setting, at the artfully arranged papers, nicely arranged, like a placemat. Notebook, center. Two ink pens, like knife and fork, and diary to the left, and a notepad with the logo, in the place where the drink would sit if it were a place setting.

The first few agenda items seemed perfunctory. The agenda moved according to the times laid out, with each of the staff members laying out their program reports. She noticed, for the first time, "Greet New Member (:22)." *Of course*, she thought to herself, *boards must stick to their agendas*. She recalled the website she read last night, You're the New Board Member: What to Expect, but wasn't finding it particularly helpful in this moment. Staring down again, she felt aimless. What if she voted the wrong way? While she took herself as a confident person, she increasingly wanted to disappear under the table.

Chief Trust Officers

Boards are the chief trust officers for an organization—they are entrusted with a mission to steward. To accomplish that, each must work toward a unified voice with the other members of the board. Yet, we live in a time when trust is in decline across the globe, especially with institutions on which the public rely. Since 1993 the annual Edelman Trust Barometer has been used to understand the degrees of trust and mistrust of institutions in the public square. Edelman is a global marketing company; they help businesses connect with their people. Their rationale for this annual undertaking is grounded in the conviction that trust "is the ultimate currency in the relationship that all institutions build with their stakeholders....Trust defines an organization's license to operate, lead and succeed." Unfortunately, democratic government, media, businesses, NGOs and nonprofits are at a new low. While 77% of those surveyed still trust their employers, many crave more social leadership from them. Shockingly, very few would live near (20%), work with (20%) or even help (30%) someone whose point of view differs from their own.[10]

With guards up at these alarming rates, we can only conjecture your boardroom and stakeholders are not immune. What does this mean? *Someone on your board distrusts someone on your board.* We are confident it is having a deteriorating effect on the impact of your organization.

A nonprofit among refugees in high-conflict areas branded itself as highly trustworthy. Less known, especially to donors and critical stakeholders, the CEO presented board reports based on one set of facts (leaving the impression that progress and results were better than they were) while staff received differing reports from program participants in the field. These reports contradicted the CEO's messages. Power struggles for truth telling ensued. As the CEO's numbers inflated, staff trust decreased. It was common for the CEO to report directly from war zones. However, when he was caught knowingly misrepresenting video footage—showing one conflict setting and saying it was another—tensions between critical stakeholders erupted. Trust was broken. Mission impact was proportionate to mission integrity, starting with the top office.

Your strategic plan cannot outpace the quality of your community's trust quotient while you are working together. The oft-repeated "Culture eats strategy for breakfast" easily gets leaders nodding in agreement, but not everything is solved by a stroke of a pen. *This* is the work of leadership—mastering a community-building mindset *while* you demonstrate the business acumen to meet strategic performance objectives. For a board, insisting on emotionally safe and predictable environments is as important as ensuring the buildings in which you work are free from termites, rusted plumbing or faulty electrical wiring. These threats may not be visible to you daily, but they are having a daily impact. And one day, when it is too late, you will think differently about small things upon which your work truly relied. Likely someone will be blamed on that day for not doing their job. We invite boards to beat everyone to it by creating a culture where safety and improvement are owned by all and supported by leadership.

Culturally Conscious Trust Is a Contact Game

We take a childhood-inspired digression. If you knew your one job was being systematically hijacked or thwarted, would you not be curious about the saboteur? If you have ever had the pleasure (or terror, depending on your playmates) of playing Pin the Tail on the Donkey, then you know how the game unfolds. To play, you need a poster-sized picture of a donkey, but without a tail. You need a strip of cardboard, fashioned into a ropelike tail, with a thumbtack or pin stuck through its widest end. One kid, wearing a blindfold, takes the thumbtack end of the donkey's tail and feels her way forward with this needle point jutting through the air, poking at anything and everything as she "pins

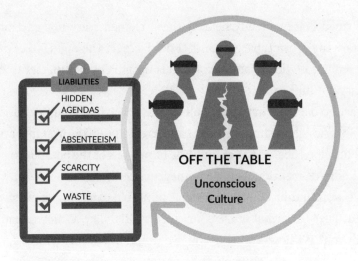

FIGURE 4.1 Unconscious Culture as a Liability

the tail on the donkey." If you are one of the other kids involved, your job is to use your sight (and common sense) to run for your life. The last thing you want is to become the "donkey."

In 1954, Gordon Allport conducted a first-of-a-kind experiment based on the "contact hypothesis," which has impacted American public policy for 70 years, as well as how boards might want to think about shaping welcoming environments.[11] The hypothesis assumed that prejudice, discrimination and bias stem from low contact. If low exposure to differences explained the anxiety and mistrust, then the natural remedy would be to increase contact. Segregation perpetuated segregation. Creating demographically integrated settings would be key. So, Allport studied racially integrated groups in the U.S. military and Northeastern urban housing projects.

The studies show changes indeed occurred. Prejudice *could* be reduced. But an odd effect also happened. Contact could *increase* prejudice! How? Unless four ingredients discovered by Allport were all part of the plan—*authority advocating for unity, equal status being affirmed, common goals being shared* and *people cooperating*—then familiarity confirmed biases already held. If these elements are not part of the diversifying project, participants should expect the opposite of prejudice reduction. Leadership's conscious design choices matter in community building.

If we go back to Pin the Tail, blindfolds thwart community building. It is not enough to simply agree that there's a problem. You must make one conscious decision at a time. The hard work of the board is to make its blindfolds mentionable and manageable.

We examine just a few potential blindfolds that break trust on a board. These are what make your culture a liability. Which one jumps out at you? Without knowing you, we would guess that whichever one stands out to you is probably the one you are feeling most strongly on your board. Let's unpack each of these briefly.

Gatekeeping, Exclusion

Gatekeeping and exclusion determine who enters, stays or exits. When a board picks a new executive director, nominates a new member or passes on a funding request, it is performing a gatekeeping function. It decides what and who is out. Boards can use term limits to help position the board to diversify its leadership. This is where board rubrics, pipelines and mentorship are important. We've also seen boards *not* use them in order to maintain the status quo and keep people out who might change things.

Groupthink, Zero Defects

Groupthink is possible when there is *high cohesion, isolated perspectives, directive leadership, lack of appraisal, homogeneity* and *an illusion of invulnerability*.[12] Self-censorship further stifles diverse views, leading to flawed outcomes. Many colleges we know have closed their doors in recent years, often saying, "We just thought we weren't vulnerable to what everyone else was facing." At one such college, high-caliber board members served because it felt purposeful. Now if one of their businesses' P&L didn't add up for over a decade, as it was with the college, they would make major cuts. But believing the mission could never fail, they continued making cosmetic cuts, postponing the deep dive until it was too late and the college closed. We've seen this happen in many organizations. And, true confessions, we get it; we have been in that seat when the last thing you want to be is the naysayer.

Bias, Self-Deception

Bias involves unnoticed tendencies influencing our views, often hidden by low exposure or self-deception. Denying biases occurs while witnessing events like an assault or showing support while opposing reforms. These biases cloud our understanding of stakeholders, hindering respectful perception. We all have biases, but for some reason we hate to admit them. There's a lost art of forgiveness in our culture. But not forgiving breeds bitterness and prevents us from seeing our stakeholders with dignity. Similar dynamics happen in boardrooms amid cultural clashes. To foster trust, acknowledging and exploring our unconscious biases is essential.

DEI Fatigue, Racial Fragility

Diversity and DEI Fatigue describe the exhaustion felt in consistently addressing cultural issues in diverse communities. Racial fragility involves discomfort with power dynamics related to race. This disinterest persists among leaders and constituents across institutions.[13] When a school noticed an increase in turnover among faculty and staff of color, they took steps to hire a diversity director and initiate multicultural programs. However, when it surveyed its community climate, the results also called for a shift in its governance mindset. Succumbing to both fatigue and fragility, the executive committee withheld the report from the full board. Avoiding acceptance of turnover patterns due to a culturally inhospitable climate, they dismissed the results as biased, woke or politically motivated. Opting for willful cultural blindfolds was easier than welcoming the voices of stakeholders negatively impacted by it.

System Blindness

System blindness occurs when individuals deeply entrenched in their roles fail to perceive broader systemic dynamics, leading to distorted decision-making.[14] A nonprofit we helped was at a crossroads. A majority of the executive director's leadership team had resigned, each citing issues with the CEO, but their complaints never went past the executive committee of the board. The next person to resign waited until after the board meeting at which he read out loud the part of the bylaws that said the executive committee was to serve at the pleasure of the board. His closing comment was that, in this organization, the board served at the pleasure of the executive committee. Within the year, the executive director resigned, and the board brought in outside consultants to assist them with changing their culture, specifically around building trust.

Privilege, Superiority

Superiority is nurtured in the belief that one's self or group is inherently superior to others. Privilege, in the context of differences like race, class and gender, signifies the unearned advantages or benefits that individuals from certain membership groups experience based solely on identity or beliefs about social status, often at the expense of marginalized or oppressed groups. A close kin to ethnocentrism and self-deception, privilege is initially natural, especially the younger or less exposed we are to groups who differ from our families and communities of origin. We invoke here again the Ghanaian proverb mentioned in the first chapter: "The woman or man who believes their mama's bread is the best in the world, has not traveled very far from home."

Removing Blindfolds That Erode Trust

This is the work of the culturally conscious board, to transform cultural liabilities into cultural assets. It is not enough to just agree, "Oh, yeah, culture is an asset." Nothing will happen. You must assess and act—one culturally conscious decision at a time. The thumbtack, in our childhood digression, is the decision. It is the thing you must get spot on for it to matter. Waiting for the masses in your outfit to get along is abdicating your culture to the whims of fears and distrust. *You* must pin liabilities down as a board. You must invest in order for assets to grow. Poking, swiping and skewering midair or, worse, the backside of one of your playmates, we all would agree, is a horrible result for a game. But when boards make decisions, it is not a game.

So, how can we remove these blindfolds? Take a moment to look ahead to Figure 4.2. What blindfolds do you recognize on your board? And what trust-building practices can you implement to ensure you are at full capacity when making decisions that impact your mission? Here are a few we suggest.

Listen with Vulnerability

Listen Actively. Think of bobbleheads—those nodding along without truly engaging. Trusted leaders foster employee trust through genuine engagement and understanding of others' perspectives. This applies equally to board members. Yet, vulnerability is vital, often hindered by the perceived status of board service. One effective practice involves reflecting back what you heard in a conversation and inviting clarification, without the need for immediate agreement.

Integrate Values. Boards entrusted with an organization's legacy rely on shared values for cohesion. In the book *Joy at Work*, Dennis Bakke, founder/CEO of AES (Applied Energy Services), outlined the four values by which he not only structured his company, but also his philanthropic philosophy: integrity, social responsibility, fairness and having fun on the job.[15] Every member embraced these values, reinforced by linking bonuses to staff ratings and emphasizing the individual's significance within the company's culture.

Cultivate Accountability. Upholding governing documents like bylaws ensures they serve as the bedrock for operational integrity and trust within a board; neglecting them undermines transparency and adherence to established protocols. We learned of a board chair who remarked, "Bylaws, schmylaws" upon being questioned about financial discrepancies in staff reports. Governing documents were an afterthought, rather than the culture-bearing standard for the systems under which their board would operate.

Require Reliability. An annual affirmation statement ensures every board member knows exactly what is expected of them. Requiring board members to sign this before committing provides accountability and transparency on several fronts—board attendance, board giving and board volunteering. Cultural differences on time and authority are important to get on the table. Discussing the why behind these commitments builds trust among members because they can rely on one another.

Invite Collegiality. Trust often eludes board assignments, neglecting the emotional connections crucial for cohesion. Rarely do members share personal stories, yet this practice fosters inclusivity, especially for non-dominant cultures. Just as trust shapes employee-supervisor relationships, it also impacts board dynamics. Conversely, lack of trust disempowers those hesitant to challenge authority. Cultural backgrounds significantly influence comfort levels in diverse boards, affecting interactions and expression of opinions. Each board member must be able to express their view without fear of reprisal.[16]

Practice Transparency. Transparency ensures alignment between values and outcomes. Sustaining it requires trust. The board of a Rwandan social-impact business consists of British, American and Rwandan members. Every month they lay everything out in the open for all to

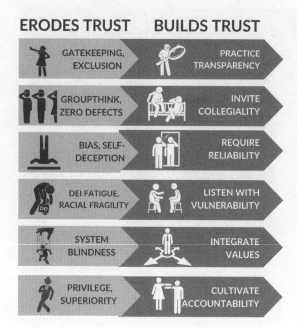

FIGURE 4.2 Moving Culture from Liability to Asset

see and question. Transparency of mission, values, numbers and challenges, along with a candid culture, keep them focused, even across cultural differences. But if the system isn't built in such a way that questions can be received and responded to, then transparency can simply become a means by which people are controlled. Corruption thrives in opacity, concealing information for personal gain, eroding trust and undermining the common good.

Society is in a time of polarization, and boards have the unique opportunity to be islands of sanctuary (and even stability), incorporating trust-based practices that strengthen decision-making and contribute to the common good. When boards make a decision, it is not a game. We prefer boards to make their decisions without any blindfolds that would hamper their capacity to see. Trust is essential for this, requiring a certain posture of humility that we'll explore together in the next chapter.

THE TAKE-HOME BOX

- Think about what experiences you have had at board meetings or retreats that have allowed you to build trust with other members. What is a common thread between them?

- Look at the trust-busting blindfolds in Figure 4.1. Which one do you recognize from your board? What story comes to mind? Which one needs to be made mentionable?

- Look at the trust-building practices. What is one practice that would help you take off that blindfold at your next board meeting?

- Are there ways in which your board funds trust-building activities among its members? Among its stakeholders? If so, what are they?

5

The Transforming Moment
Begins with Humility

Something there is that doesn't love a wall,

That wants it down.

ROBERT FROST[17]

"Breathe, Crystal," she told herself. "These people might not know you, but you can make some assumptions on how they might vote on issues." She knew how accomplished they all were. Phil, the board chair, was a former NFL hopeful (until he blew out his knee), a commercial real estate broker and widely respected in town. He was sometimes called Colonel by friends who knew of his National Guard service. Michael was a labor attorney, recently appointed as chief council for Catholic Health Systems. Jemma was one of Sierra's business professors and one of the catalysts to City Farm's decision to bypass some of the well-worn poverty alleviation strategies and experiment with the B-Corp concept. B-Corps were confronting the systemic inequities of business, finance and wealth and reframing business to expand economic opportunity. Crystal got the impression Jemma hadn't been to board meetings in a while but didn't know why. Thomas, another board member absent tonight, was in banking. He and his siblings ran a family foundation in the city, built on four generations of wealth from the now-defunct Bethlehem Steel plant in town. Sam, another businessman, owned numerous car dealerships and sponsored most city events. City Farm was fueled by innovation, resourceful people and a lot of grit, all of which seemed to match Sierra's character ever since Crystal knew her as a child.

Crystal felt intimidated. She was a community nutritionist and an administrator, not someone with experience leading an organization with high finance plans and lots of moving parts. She was there for Sierra and the neighborhood, she told herself. And in the recesses of her mind, she remembered the words Gramma used to say to her: "Know who you are, where you come from and what you stand for." She'd take that wisdom with her.

Phil, on the other hand, was incredibly pleased. He prided himself on efficient meetings and was grateful for Sierra's professionalism as the executive director. To save time, he and Sierra decided which items were most important to discuss. Together, they resolved matters easily, without bothering the entire board. Knowing how busy everyone was, he didn't want to bother people with too much unnecessary work. In his commercial real estate company, he knew how to cut through the trivial and keep things moving to get the job done.

Serving on the board and celebrating the excellent work being done in the community through City Farm was a breath of fresh air for him. It was easy work. The most contentious thing they had been through as an organization was making the decision to move Sierra from volunteer founder to executive director. Sierra was thorough in her work and really didn't need the board to do much except raise funds through their network, and they were all good at that. This is why *bringing in Crystal* was a surprise to Phil. He didn't really feel they needed more do-gooders. They needed more money and connections if this $11 million site expansion and the new move to Buffalo were going to become a reality. Sierra felt it was important to nominate Crystal, so Phil accommodated her nomination, still unsure of what value she'd bring.

Humility: A Demanding Posture

We have come to the heart of the matter—an appreciative view of your board's progress in its personal and organizational humility. Only a board so grounded is likely to look within and beyond itself to absorb messages about itself that arise from its performance, people processes and programs results. In the last chapter we looked at the liabilities that arise from low trust in relationships. You don't want low trust on your board. So, what is the posture that is needed to catalyze that trust dynamic in such a way that it strengthens the cultural consciousness of groups and their members? Humility.

But let us be real—humility is demanding. It requires something of you. It does not let you off the hook with excuses of weakness nor an inflated view of yourself, your capacities or even your view of difficult and unsavory tasks. If humility detects you are equal to the moment, humility also offers a supply of fortitude to fulfil its demands. Bob Andringa, author of *Nonprofit Board Answer Book* and former president of one of the nation's largest higher education associations, found himself looking into a mirror. It came in the form of a study on faith-based communities, where sociologists asked 1,500 participants questions about why churches often divide along racial lines. They published the study in the book *Divided by Faith*. What they uncovered was a startling insight: Individualism—whether it wears church clothes or golf shirts at 11.00 on Sunday morning, the hour Martin Luther King Jr. called the most segregated hour in America—is enabled by an underlying cultural insistence on an individualistic view of humanity and institutions. Bob made some changes. He changed churches. He invited friends, staff and then his board to read the study. New committees, new programs and a first-ever national conference on diversity were launched (and continue to this day!). Because humility makes demands on us, Bob translated his position and capacity for governance—systems, structures, and policies and strategy—into capacity for social transformation. Talk is cheap, and he knew it. We all know those who have used their position and power for the exact opposite.

Humility, from *humus,* literally comes from the terms *earth* and *on the ground.* A "grounded person" is implied, but grounded in *what* exactly? Does this mean groveling at someone's feet? Is this where I become a doormat to my board chair, the donors, the angry clients who want the showers and food to be hotter? We can see how *on the ground* might awaken your worse fears about humility's demands.

Our bias is that it is difficult to know ourselves fully in isolation; humility requires self-recognition, an understanding of our own viewpoints and biases, while we also recognize the limits of our self-perception. It's the "aha" moment in Pin the Tail when you realize you'll continue flailing until you listen to the voices of your friends, pointing you in the right direction.

Some of our most cherished lessons about humility are not derived from textbooks and dictionaries but from listening. Jennifer highlights the summer she spent listening to nearly 50 Rwandan textile workers from three different predominantly female cooperatives in Kigali, Rwanda. The cooperatives epitomize a self-governing and self-determining deliberative body in which each member's livelihood rises and falls at the same rate as others within the community. She asked, "What is humility?" While she learned a lot from these industrious women, over and over she heard that humility is kept grounded with and by humanity, recognizing the dignity of another. One leader offered: "[Humility is] somebody that has humility. It is that kind of person that shows respect, humanity to everyone; whether those younger than them, or those that are older than them. So, you show respect to every individual."[18]

Barry Rowan is a board member we deeply respect. He is a Harvard Business School graduate who spent his entire career serving in C-suite roles. Instrumental in building and transforming numerous multimillion-dollar businesses (with one selling for $10 billion), his leadership experience spans both private and public companies. Based on his belief in giving back, Rowan serves on both for-profit and nonprofit boards, mentors young leaders and leads international study trips. While he has been in leadership of numerous companies, he comes alive when talking about his board service in organizations at work in various cultural contexts. On failure, he says there are only "two ways to fail: to fail to try and to fail to learn."[19] The way Rowen models humility requires a posture of learning, perspective-taking and a constant reminder that this social impact work is about something greater than ourselves.

Our consciousness of our own culture and that of others deepens as our learning accumulates. Some of that deepening comes from the mistakes and failures Rowan mentions. In our highly reactive social media environment, organizations are canceled or punished for unwitting mistakes, some of which might just as easily have been opportunities for growth. As Edgar Schein, organizational culture scholar, asserts, we must be able to "nurture change as a perpetual process, not just as a one-time success or failure."[20] Humility allows us to accept uncertainty while remaining open to learning, attentive to what others know of a situation that we cannot see. And humility allows us to recognize when our biases can affect our analysis of a situation.

Choosing Humility Over Arrogance

We admit, the path of humility, down which a board may be led, is not the easier path, not by a long stretch. Humility's path requires attention and courage. It requires conflict even. Humility anticipates it can be wrong. It knows there's potential to miss some vital detail significant to a stakeholder who relies on the board to get it right. If morale, donations and your building's upkeep are slumping, humility makes room to consider one's part in why things are as they are. These slumping states may reflect "a failure of imagination." If that sounds exaggerated, maybe a bit harsh, consider it in its context of a congressional investigation in which U.S. Senator Clinton Anderson asked Frank Borman, the astronaut who had to investigate the ground explosion that claimed the lives of three fellow astronauts, "What caused the fire?" Frank Borman responded, "A failure of imagination." By ourselves, we are certainly prone to a failure of imagination, but humbly acknowledging we need what is on the table and what is off the table is a conversation we must host for our mission to succeed.

It is mind-boggling how many leaders are clinically diagnosed narcissists. The 2021 study in *Leadership Quarterly* reported that narcissists become CEOs faster than those who do not share those markers. This was true independent of the type of firm.[21] Narcissism is the antithesis to humility, the exact trait needed for social impact and nonprofit organizations that work in an increasingly globalized world. On *your* board, the type of culture you have will be partly indicated by the type of CEO you hire. Few boards assess personality traits that indicate narcissism. Who you have in leadership matters for the trust-building culture you are creating. If the leadership is trusted by a diverse group of stakeholders who believe the leadership will represent and advocate for them, then that may be more important than the demographics of the board.

This is important. Many times, when we advocate for a culturally conscious board, members betray their misunderstanding of the task by referring to tokenized checklists: "We just don't have a diverse enough pipeline. Can you help us develop one?" Lily Zheng explores this in *DEI Deconstructed*. Confusing demographic diversity with adoption of culturally conscious dispositions and practices is problematic. Demographically diverse boards that fail to act conscientiously with their stakeholders are bound to fail at the same rate as boards that may be demographically homogenous, yet absent-minded about the role culture plays in decision-making. If the membership's combined awareness generates culturally deficient decisions, its demographic makeup hardly matters. Trust is the key ingredient with stakeholders.

What communities are you able to build trust with that are important to the success of your organization? What kind of person might you need on your board to better reach those communities? Most importantly, what kind of board does this vision of community require you to become? How many revolving-door recruitment stories would surface if we asked, "Why did you leave?" Study after study supports well-manicured recruitment brochures that cannot supplant the neglected-hygiene factors responsible for high turnover and alienation in workplaces. As the saying goes, people do not quit jobs; they quit managers. We would add: they quit cultures too.

So you have a role in setting a different kind of table. You welcome people of mission-centered integrity to claim their seats as guests. They are guests of a mission—voiceless, paper-thin, devoid of power to enact anything—unless they fulfill their fiduciary pledge, conscious of each stakeholder, and give voice to that mission. The way in which you make each decision is the same way a host embodies hospitality and welcome. So bear with us, as we venture into that way of being—the mindsets necessary to approach the table and ensure that every voice is heard.

Humility: A Way of Being

Just as there are practices to build trust, there are mindsets to lean into that cultivate humility. As you read through these brief descriptions, consider which mindset you personally want to embody at your next board meeting.

Civility. A culturally conscious board is likely made up of people who want to make a difference, often people whose professional lives may require others to listen to them, rather than the other way around. Strong convictions are expected. But it is a fact that 98% of people experience rudeness in the workplace.[22] This only affirms that boards will also experience the tendency to demonize others, silence, shame or even control committee assignments. Humility calls for civility. The Seattle Organization for Prostitution Survivors is an organization founded, led and staffed by survivors. Many on their team have experienced deep trauma. Civility is a must. And so they start every board meeting with norms, laying out the values by which they expect to engage in dialogue. By assuming this mindset, they allow deeper trust to be formed.

Curiosity. Curiosity is often seen as a trait of those seeking information. What if we instead think of it as a powerful trait of those seeking connection—to ideas and people? Seventy percent of nonprofits have at least one board member of color, 34% have at least one board member with a disclosed disability, and 44% have at least one board member who identifies as LGBTQ+.[23] Think of the life stories around your boardroom table. Becoming curious is a humble posture and, again, allows for deeper trust to be formed.

Dignity. Recognizing the dignity of others is a prerequisite for becoming culturally conscious as a person and as a board member, especially when working among diverse constituencies. In *Leading with Dignity*, Donna Hicks considers dignity to be *the* missing ingredient in conflict resolution, whether that be in a classroom or in a war zone. Board-room conflicts are no fun, especially when those off-the-table items get moved onto the table. But recognizing the dignity of another can allow you both to remain at the table.

Empathy. Innovation, engagement and inclusion all increase with an empathetic leader who possesses the ability to understand and share the feelings of another.[24] Empathy starts with asking, If I were in her position, what would I want/need/do? And by taking an active interest not only in board members' lives, but also in the other stakeholders attached to the organization. When is the last time you heard from a program participant, staff person or donor at your board meeting? Understanding why people invest in, work with and receive from your organization allows you to be more empathetic.

Flexibility. We reflect here on a college event in which 50 local Spanish-speaking leaders came for a dialogue. Brochures of campus summer programs were placed on each table. Running out of space on the tables, the host removed a brochure for a program she deemed cost-prohibitive to the guests. A junior staff member from the Dominican Republic challenged her to let the guests decide what is cost-prohibitive. It was a transformative moment, revealing biases in the group. Authentic apologies given, the brochure stayed and catalyzed a shift in focus to the guests. A Spanish-speaking board member became the host. The entire event was hosted in Spanish, rather than English. The event became cherished for its inclusivity. Removing blinders and being flexible served the college's mission far better.

Hospitality. Ancient Greeks viewed hospitality as a virtuous mindset, not a customer service transaction. Their word for this mindset of readiness, *xenophilos*, literally means "lover of strangers." This mind-set exists yet today as a moral, spiritual and social expectation. Rather than a transactional customer service process, it reflects a kind of vir-tuous person whose posture is welcoming, attentive, protective and generous. At a board meeting, it requires ensuring that every new board member knows they belong. As they arrive in their own cultural clothing, they are welcomed to the boardroom table because their voice is needed. '

Integrity. We're both parents who often tell our children that character is who you are when no one is looking. It is possessing integrity where you live, outside of the commitments you make. And that requires accountability. It's natural to put on some pretense when in a new setting. But are the values you uphold privately brought with you to the boardroom table? And when you come together collectively, does your board take time to ensure that your board policies and structures point back to the values and commitments by which you operate as an organization? Does the board have its own accountability structures in place to ensure the integrity of its collective decision-making?

The Host Models Humility

As humility grows, so does trust. Your board culture becomes an asset. What has been unmentionable is made mentionable and even mendable. But if these transforming capacities hide in plain sight, like lost eyeglasses, cell phones or car keys—tools we cannot live without for long periods of time if we do not want to get lost or lose connection—then how do we find them? How do they help us put it on the table, to make mentionable? How do you host such a table where culture is an asset? (Figure 5.1)

It is true that ultimately the chair of the board has a lot of say in whether or not your board will become culturally conscious, modeling humility and building trust. When you consider how to host such a table, it can become easy to look to someone else to lead the way. We'll just leave it to the person at the head of the table, right? Often, the "hostess with the mostest" is the inviter or the one holding a prominent

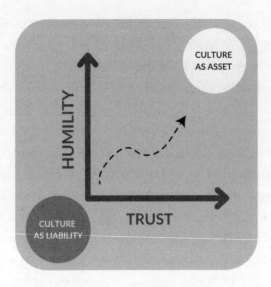

FIGURE 5.1 Asset and Liability Effect

position at the table. However, sometimes it's the individuals with the loudest voices or the strongest opinions who leave a profound impact on the gathering, shaping the conversation, tearing away at any trust that has been built. These instances can sometimes resemble hostage situations, where the emotional tone of the group is dictated by the angriest or saddest person present. In these moments, true leadership is required.

Annie, a retired sports, entertainment and healthcare marketing executive from Virginia's Hampton Roads, fostered a welcoming supper club where neighbors shared stories and meals. Shifts in the political climate also shifted the atmosphere, turning once-pleasant discussions sour and confrontational. Despite Annie's attempts to guide the conversations, a vocal few steered the group off its intended path. Reflecting on her Southern upbringing, she recognized media influences and vulnerabilities in society's either/or mindsets. Contemplating her role as host, she considered setting boundaries or discontinuing. But the COVID pandemic beat her to it—in-person meetings were suspended.

When the world reopened and the group sought to resume meetings at her home, Annie declined. Determined to participate in change, in solidarity with her wide-ranging family and friendship circles, she formed a new table group, centered more consistently with social and racial justice. By the time Russ interviewed her for her story, she had been meeting for an unbroken 197 weeks. (By the way, her real name is not Annie. The host in this story assumed the name of a caretaker in her Carolina childhood family home to honor Annie Ruth. The real Annie, having little power to change the unequal and unjust social structures, nevertheless modeled grace, power, dignity and welcome.)[25]

We could *all* be more like Annie when we host at our boardroom tables. It is not just the responsibility of the chair. By embracing the responsibility of the host, you elevate the conversation and draw attention to the treatment of individuals in the room.

We understand the reservations and potential pushback—the rubber stamper's objections, the pragmatist's skepticism or the chair's initial resistance. But it takes courage to shift the atmosphere, and often less courageous or engaged individuals secretly appreciate the change. By leading the conversation into deeper waters when it's clear the board is surface skimming in order to avoid hurting feelings or naming poor performance, you render service in the very way that a host or hostess drives past awkward silences or a guest's sudden (and mortifying) burp. Sometimes, all a board needs is for someone to give a damn.

So, as the next board meeting approaches, with its chance to transform conversations from superficial banter to something substantial, the question, Who is the host? evolves to the question, Who is going to *be* the host? Your willingness to make the unmentionable mentionable may be uncomfortable at times, but it will benefit you and the board as a community and increase your capacity to rely on judgments born from the risk of truth telling, integrity and lived experience.

Be conscious. Speak your voice. As Representative John Lewis's legacy urges, get in some "good trouble, necessary trouble."[26] Organizational silence is unbecoming of fiduciary officers, and it's damning of boards if they lead with the unexamined weight of these liabilities. So take the time to examine them. You are giving your time, treasure and talent. Humility's path will require a transformation, of you, your board and the fulfillment system upon which your stakeholders rely. But you promised them you would deliver.

THE TAKE-HOME BOX

- What is one mindset you would like to cultivate in a deeper way at your next board meeting?

- Consider the makeup of your board. What voice might be missing from your boardroom table that is needed for your mission?

- Remember a place or moment where you felt you were a guest in your work or organization. And when you were the host. How did the experiences differ?

- When was the last time you heard from a beneficiary, a staff person, a donor at your board meeting?

- Is there an area of your board culture that has not been addressed that you want to give voice to?

6

Claim Your Seat,
Lift Every Voice

The Board Culture Placemat

*Lift every voice and sing, Till earth and heaven ring, Ring with
the harmonies of Liberty; Let our rejoicing rise High as the
list'ning skies, Let it resound loud as the rolling sea.*

JAMES WELDON JOHNSON[27]

"Last agenda item," Phil called out. "We've been given the
opportunity to purchase a building in the city of Buffalo. It'll
allow us to expand to a second site in downtown Buffalo. And
get this—it is ours for only $1! The only stipulation is that the
city is requiring us to create a homeless shelter as part of the
occupancy use. We've been talking about expansion and I'm
very excited about it. This seems like a no-brainer."

Crystal had only received the agenda two hours ahead of time,
so she quickly perused the summary. It all sounded good. God
knows there was an ever-increasing homeless population in the
city. And then, Michael asked, "Phil, it sounds amazing, but how
do we pay for the care and maintenance of the building after
its purchase...that's not going to be $1." Phil assuaged both
concerns at the same time: "We would not be considering this

generous offer from the city if it wasn't in our best interest." All heads nodded in affirmation, with eyes on the clock nearing 8:00 p.m.

"Phil, I have a question," announced Crystal. Her own voice colliding with the board's readiness to adjourn sounded like cymbal clashes to her. She felt like she was awakening everyone from their rightful slumber. But she urged on. As if all were in suspended animation, except her, she posed her question, a question about a budget item that didn't seem to make sense: "Is a homeless shelter the mission of City Farm?"

Everyone just seemed to stare back at her as if she had done something that was on what Gramma used to describe as the "naughty list" and the "oughty list" (the things you can't say out loud and the things you ought to say out loud, even if it rocks the boat to say them). She sensed the boat had just gotten rocked a bit.

Michael was bemused that Crystal had just broken an unwritten cardinal rule of this board. It was the "Thou shalt not speak as a new board member for at least six meetings" rule. He adjusted his seat and sat up a bit straighter, fully ready for what was likely to occur next. Phil, trying not to be annoyed, simply responded, "I'm just reporting on the opportunity for tonight. There will be discussion at a later time."

Board meetings were about to get a tad more interesting.

The Board Culture Placemat

From ancient times, placemats of natural materials were used not only to preserve the table beneath from spills and heat, but as decorative ornaments to indicate wealth and status. In medieval times, as individual seats replaced shared benches, placemats also took on more decorative and ceremonial purposes. As seating arrangements displaced "first come, first served" mindsets, proper etiquette and table manners were required for the setting of the table. Our development of the Board Culture Placemat is a nod to the intentionality with which conscious table culture was held in esteem.

As board coaches for the Murdock Charitable Trust, we have learned to nonjudgmentally respect the various predicaments our clients face and instead focus on the action path ahead. Since we could never be as smart as the client about their situation, we "coach the person, not the problem."[28] As coaches, we trust that our questions do the heavy lifting. That is why we created The Board Culture Placemat, a tool to help you claim your seat and use your voice to make the unmentionable mentionable and mendable. The Board Culture Placemat contains five essential conversations every culturally conscious board must have—on identity, intention, invitation, investment and impact. View the statements in each section of the placemat as conversation starters to help your board think through each stage of its organization's delivery system. We rely on this model repeatedly to amplify the notion that what we do, most always, proceeds from *who* we are.

Because most boards have very little time together and some priorities around value and policy clarification are sometimes only discussed when situations or annual events trigger the conversation, this tool selects several critical conversation topics that boards can explore together.[29] We aim to make the manners you practice mentionable and mendable. Instead of a Take-Home Box as at the end of each earlier chapter, we offer the conversation-starting true-or-false statements for you to consider, along with some questions you and your board can reflect on together.

As you navigate the five essential capacity-building conversations we propose, the benefit will become manifest within months,

THE BOARD PLACEMAT

INTENTION
- We consult mission, vision, values during decisions.
- We examine policies for fairness, equity and inclusion.
- We expect status reports on the mission-based promise to stakeholders.
- We are convinced our theory of change makes a difference.
- We orchestrate our progress through a strategic plan.

IMPACT
- We measure our efforts by evidence-based outcomes regularly.
- We avoid dependency and parental mindsets.
- We compare results to stated intentions, promises.
- We harvest learning after events, milestones, fails, wins.
- We recognize, celebrate, encourage efforts of the team.

CulturallyConsciousBoard.com

INVITATION
- We leverage our mission and story to attract stakeholders.
- We recruit members who add capacity, not merely fit.
- We glean stakeholder feedback to lift our cultural blindfolds
- We embody a partnership of equals, a participatory approach.
- We cultivate diverse candidate pools when recruiting.

INVESTMENT
- We require budget priorities to reflect mission intent.
- We fund evidence-based efforts-to-outcome strategies.
- We ask "How can we afford it (or afford not to)?" instead of "Can we afford it?"
- We model our mission engagement by participating financially.
- We build board capacity through cultural mentors and advisors.

IDENTITY
- We reaffirm our origin story.
- We make values mentionable.
- We align our walk with our talk.
- We honor stakeholders' identities, while true to ours.
- We make time to know our members' stories.

SCAN ME
DOWLOAD, PRINT

SET THE TABLE 1 MARK TRUE OR FALSE.

2 COMPARE DIFFERENCES.

3 DECIDE: START, STOP, SUSTAIN

FIGURE 6.1 The Board Culture Placemat

evidenced in the explicit use of culture as an asset for your mission. It requires a combination of observation, active participation and relationship building. It requires a certain mindset grounded in humility that induces trust. Remember that boardroom culture will evolve. It can vary from one board to another. Remaining at the table is half the battle. Recognizing what is on, off and beyond the table is the second half. There is no Take-Home Box for this chapter. Rather, let us begin the placemat conversation.

Five Essential Conversations

In Part Three, we explore a conscious-raising tool that surfaces and transforms the unmentionable assumptions that leave a board operating at half capacity. When your board, in humility, assesses its unconscious culture, it makes the unmentionable manageable. This becomes the working, conscious, part of the board's decision-making capacity. The good news: the use of this placemat is not a "one and done" board retreat exercise, but rather a new muscle to exercise. Our questions are not magic, nor superior to your own. Instead, we have summarized a significant body of board development wisdom in each one. We have shaped them around a logic model that organizes around a promise-fulfillment process. We are confident these questions will lead to more questions, different ones that are right for your board and its context.

We would like to hear how your board uses this. Tell us about the questions your board comes up with, that we have not asked. Write us at team@culturallyconsciousboard.com to share your board's Board Culture Placemat story!

7

Identity

The wise attend to the inner truth of things
and are not fooled by outward appearances.

LAO TZU[30]

That vacant chair, Michael thought to himself. The traffic light stared back an eternal red. He drummed his fingers on the leather steering wheel...pinky to thumb, over and over...drumming...willing the light to change, as with Jedi powers. That vacant chair. He was still thinking about it on his drive back through town, back to Buffalo. It was only a 27-minute drive. But in some ways, what he did every first Tuesday was worlds apart from so much of his life. At least, in comparison to his life today.

Michael had not always lived in such fine settings. In many ways, he was still unused to it, as his wife, Sharon, might attest to friends during their every-third-Tuesday trivia nights at the neighborhood pub. On this side of his life, it was all weekly lawn mowing, BBQs and dog walking. The twins had taken over the family schedule ever since they were 11-year-olds, with one a rising swim star, the other a first-chair violinist.

The stability and rhythm of his current world was what he never imagined possible as a child in Liberia. There were still

77

moments when he'd wake in the middle of the night in a sweat, the fight-or-flight mode triggered by a tree branch hitting the window. It was like it was yesterday. He remembers the warm breeze outside their modest home in Monrovia and the feel of the bitterball and cassava leaves in his hand from the small plot of land. But mostly he remembers increased tensions, quiet whisperings around the family table, where they'd all gather around the one small radio to hear rumors of Charles Taylor invading from the west to overthrow President Doe. His family was for liberation.

His parents were from New York, fell in love in college during a Vietnam War protest. They went to Liberia with the Peace Corps and fell in love with the country. Choosing to go against the capitalist grain, they started a farm outside of Monrovia, working cooperatively with many in the village. They had more than the locals, but not much. Michael and his baby brother were educated at home, with tutoring provided by missionaries at St. Peter's Lutheran church. At age 15, he only knew Liberia as his home. He was aware that being white gave him certain privileges, as much as his parents fought against this. When there was a crisis or rationing, he knew his family could always go to the embassy for help. But that day, gathered around the table, he sensed a fear in his parents he hadn't felt before. He heard his parents whispering at night about leaving, for the kids' safety. And so they began to pack, but not in time.

The government's soldiers came that night. Searching for rebels, they killed indiscriminately. Hundreds of people fled to St. Peter's, next to their home. His parents grabbed their bags and began to load the car, shoving him and his brother in. A sound like a branch hitting the window became a cacophony of bullets against the side of the car. His mother screamed as his father's suddenly lifeless body fell on her. The color of his skin was of no protection in that moment. It was all a blur for days after that. Somehow they got to the embassy and were granted passage to the United States; he left Liberia's warm coastal breeze for the frigid winters of Buffalo. And so he found himself in Baker Park, the childhood home of his mother.

He felt alone in high school. Kids spread rumors that his dad must have been a CIA agent, killed in action, or a crazy mission-ary, because why else would a kid like him ever live in "Africa." "It's a continent, not a country," he'd mutter back, longing for the friendships from his village. He soon found escape and community in books. They fueled his imagination and gave him language for the loss he felt. Books led him far away from Baker Park to college and law school, until he returned to care for his ailing mother.

And then one day, something drew him back to the old neigh-borhood and apartment. His former mentors mentioned a new influx of refugees from Liberia living in Baker Park, who could often be found at a community garden called City Farm. He found himself driving back down Route 62, walking the old streets until he found it. And he couldn't believe it. Nestled among lettuce, tomatoes and cucumbers were cassava roots and bitterball. As he watched community members, including new refugees, harvesting, he suddenly pictured the farm his parents had started that had employed and fed so many in his commu-nity in Monrovia. Before he knew it, he was asking if he could help. They put him in the garden. It would be two years before one of the Liberian farmers mentioned to Sierra, the executive director, that Michael was a lawyer. How did she not know that

after he showed up faithfully for two years, every month, weed-
ing beds, spreading donated horse manure and occasionally
planting some lemongrass?

And so he joined the board, but this was different from other
boards he served with. Yes, Sierra needed his legal expertise,
which was certainly lacking on the board, but it was his way
of being, his humility, she'd say, that allowed him to weed the
garden one minute and advocate for immigration rights and
food policy the next. He knew how to walk in both worlds, and
that was a gift sorely lacking on their board. The board began to
change when he arrived. His perspective as a refugee allowed
the board to do the perspective-taking it had been lacking. Sure,
Sierra had the heart and drive, as any founder should, but there
were blind spots that Michael began to open their eyes to. And
one night it got heated. It all had to do with that empty chair.

Why So Serious?

If a board is going to be blamed, then it might as well decide in advance
for what it most wants to be blamed. Odd thought, we know. But think
along with us more deeply. If a board that seeks to master culturally
conscious decision-making knows there is the possibility its decisions
will be scrutinized, resisted and misinterpreted, it might allocate the
time and conversation to define what is really, *really* worth it. Too
often, it is only when the moment of truth comes that a board dis-
covers its policy guidelines are ambiguous, its branding scheme is not
fully thought through for relevance and reception with demographic
audiences that may care it exists. When we least expect it, we may
have to account for who we are and why that matters to what we do, no
matter the reception.

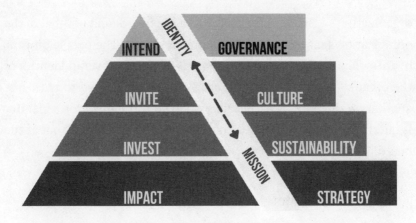

FIGURE 7.1 Identity in Board Capacity Building

In Figure 7.1, we see the role of identity in the board capacity-building process. As intentions are expressed through a governance-informed fulfillment chain and this leads to impact, we convey the centrality and reach of identity. It pertains to everything you do. As the board is, the board does. The intersection between your board's origin story and that of your members is foundational to how you do your work. It is an expression of who you are. It is the mosaic of characteristics shaping your unique sense of self, as well as the membership groups to which you belong and through which you express yourself.

A serious spiritual purpose resides at the heart of every organization. Organizations fill a gap. They make change happen. They work to make a difference. While other organizations and agencies may exist, working on similar challenges, your organization has its own distinctive origin story. It has its preferred future, its theory of change, its stakeholders, its capital constraints. This blend shapes itself into a recognizable identity that sometimes boils down to just a few words, such as *mission, vision, values* and *mandates.*

Safeguarding the organization's identity is crucial to everything else board members undertake in their service tenure. Your organization's identity is the purview of the board (and not that of the organization's marketing or development effort). The people on your board—their stories, their experiences—shape the overall identity of the organization. Do you know each other well enough to trust one another on the hard days? Because when your organization's identity is questioned, fingers will not point at the marketing team, but at the board.

Reputation: It's Out of Your Hands

We are both parents of young adults, Generation Z to be clear. In *every* generation before theirs, communication operated through branches of connected wires, not too far removed from the image of two tin cans joined by a string, eardrums straining to pick up vibrations. It took time for messages to travel. Newspapers and headline news followed this same time-lagged contortion of messaging. Back in the day, if it was in the newspapers or came out of the mouth of Walter Cronkite, you could trust it. (Oh! If you don't know who Walt-....Never mind. You already googled it.) A man wept with a nation when a president was shot. They had time to resonate, to calm, to unify. It took time, trust and even blind trust in the institutions that could mirror back a good cry.

Our kids are different. They are not defective, nor stricken with "the snobbery of chronology,"[31] as C. S. Lewis once described it of those whose criticism of the current moment is based on their ignorance of what has passed. But rather, with a thumb press and a swipe, they buckle themselves in to a hypersensory cultural hive that sees and feels everything at the same time, upvoting and downvoting what hurts too much or what's just plain "Nope!" They have thousands and thousands of Cronkites! They cry together, immediately, as a school shooting takes place—they are *in* classrooms when those moments occur, as their own school goes on alert and they instinctively begin "Run, Hide, Fight" procedures.

They know the world in a way that is jarringly different from every generation that precedes them. They are culturally conscious in a manner that is akin to postapocalyptic survival readiness. They feel threatened by institutions, so they keep their eye on them, as just one of 50 or 60 social dials they scan constantly without registering anything too deeply, instead accumulating a sense of the collective mind, so that when the call to action comes, they move *en masse*. They are big data people, and it is loud where they live. They tone it down by dividing the world into a simple binary—is it helping or hurting?

These Z's do not mess around. They are serious about everything and light about it at the same time, because something else is coming in a few minutes they will need to weigh in on. If your message is hurting, they notice you. And visibility is never free. In fact, you have to pay *something* if you understand and value the role your organization's identity plays in theirs. They personally identify with the channels— friends, celebrities, organizations are all equal to them—that they permit to shape the moral, community-affirming, diversity-assumed ecosystem they are curating, one like and subscribe at a time. And if you have been granted permission to be in their space, they are waiting to have their own identity confirmed, their own values stirred up and made manifest back to them in the mirror of the cacophony that is their personal social space. You must be authentic about who you are. The wireless generation—perhaps you have caught on that this is not just about Gen Z, but about everyone who sees everything at once—is passionate to hold systems accountable for injustice.

But, we realize, herein lies the tension. Some may push back: "You can't make long-term sustainable decisions based on opinions that may change with each like or dislike. Does this mean our organization must be all things to all people? Anything goes?" No. You must keep the mission at the forefront. There may be times when you will have to pound the table and exclaim, "This does not serve the mission." There may be times when identity and values do not align, that some may have to leave the table.

You see, identity and reputation are not the same: When nuns serving as nurses in a clinic in Syria were asked why they offered the same compassionate care to wounded Syrian soldiers that they offered to civilians wounded by the actions of those soldiers, these fervent Catholic workers explained, "The sisters don't do this because of who they are. We do this because of who we are."[32] The answer from these medical workers highlights how identity shapes decisions. It shows how identity becomes reputation. It affects how it can become a feature of an organization's brand or its story.

Scholars who study personality make a distinction between identity and reputation.[33] Identity is the story we tell ourselves about ourselves. It is internal and intrinsic. It reveals who we are, our core being, values and beliefs. Reputation is the story others tell about us based on how others perceive our actions, behavior and interactions with the world. Only one of these can a board influence. An organization's identity is always an inside job that informs the core mission, vision, values, culture and brand. And it is probably one of the most underutilized assets in a board's governance repertoire.

Harden the Targets: Identity Theft in the Boardroom

Maybe you have seen those warnings from financial institutions and web providers that say identity theft is on the rise. They describe the methods used and the disruption it causes to ordinary people who never thought identity crime could happen to them. Practicing heightened vigilance while online is the suggested remedy. As annoying and tedious as typing in passwords and resetting log-ins may be, we can appreciate why we must do them. The advice from security experts is to "harden your targets" and assume a posture of vigilance.

Your organization's identity is one of its most critical assets. A boardroom table, just like a dining room table shared among friends, is hardly the place we would expect we need to have our guard up against identity theft. And yet when a board contradicts its own mission, it does not *drift*, it *decides*. With eyes wide open, the board is either in direct service of its mission or in direct contradiction.

Opportunity

There is nothing like a grand opportunity to cause a board to lose its collective mind. Any opportunity placed before a board that creates such urgency that the team's due diligence instincts are dulled is too good to be true. In fact, it is not even good. It is bad for the board because it is bad for the mission. Here again, the emphasis is on the inseparable connection between the organization's mission-shaped identity and its mission-guarding officers, the board.

Opportunities, when left unexamined, can be detrimental to a board's effectiveness. Some opportunities dazzle with suggestions that shortcuts to success and impact exist. If it is too good to be challenged, or tabled until proven missional, then it is too good for your board to consider. Nothing should be sold to a group of fiduciary officers without a thorough and meticulous evaluation and verification process. In such moments, the mission requires a guardian, a voice to speak up on its behalf. This is especially true if most of the decision team is seemingly all for the initiative.

Risk

Ironically, risk is on an equal footing with opportunities, from a board's decision-making perspective. Both can hijack the fiduciary sensibilities of ordinarily measured and thoughtful boards. Seldom do the embedded risks to an organization's integrity or sustainability broadcast themselves as problematic. Breakthroughs in brain imaging over the last few decades have increasingly made neuroscience insights accessible to the average person. One of the easiest doctrines of brain behavior reduces to "fight, flight or freeze." (Some add "or fawn," the instinct to appease or minimize danger.) These reactions to threats make sense to most people. Danger awakens the mind, braces us for action. A staid, formal boardroom discussion hardly gives off signals that danger is lurking. And then a public relations disaster causes an organization to freeze and then go into fight or flight mode, but what gets lost in the process? The devils are indeed hiding in the details.

Donors and Partners

It is idealistic, if not politically naïve, to assume donors, donations and grants are neutral in their impact on the direction of social impact organizations. Leaving this assumption unstated perpetuates this naïveté. Leaving it unmentionable or unquestioned when it may be happening right before the eyes of a board, in its agenda and deliberations, weakens a board's fiduciary muscles. Because dollars matter, those who donate them matter. And what matters to donors, including their biases and agendas, can sway organizations in their decision-making. Every gift must undergo a process to ensure it advances the organization's purpose and impact.

We interviewed a grant manager who works for one of the largest foundations in the United States. Self-identifying as an atheist, she described a contradictory trend in the funding of international NGOs: Due to both personal experiences and historical cases of faith traditions being the source of harm in certain justice areas, such as gender equity, racial justice and LGBTQ rights, large institutional philanthropy tends to steer clear of faith-based organizations. Yet, she also acknowledged that it is faith-based organizations that represent a third of the 50 largest nonprofits in the United States and 40% of the international NGO sector.[34]

Hope International's CEO, one of the top microfinance companies in the world, considered fidelity to identity when a donor gift, the largest ever, came with the stipulation that references to faith had to be muted in their social impact efforts. To deny its foundations and aspirations would be to deny its capacity to deliver its promise. This denial was as unsustainable as any other decision that weakened capacity. And it became a board discussion where they decided mission infidelity could not be purchased. They declined the gift.

Conflicting values will always exist within the transformation sector. We point to a tug-of-war that can take place when opportunity, bias and power dynamics come into play on the boardroom table. How a board decides, when conflicting values and shiny new objects are before them, will test the alignment of its members. Mature deliberation that respectfully interrogates complexity and contradiction may be uncomfortable, but it may also cultivate an island of sanctuary in a wider society desperate for examples of collaborative integrity to a cause. We challenge boards to harden the targets described above, to protect themselves from inadvertent identity theft by validating the demands inherent in their missions, values and aspirations.

Talking Through Identity Using the Placemat

In the chapters that follow, we fashioned a series of statements that are either true or false descriptions of your organization. Take a moment to review each. You are invited to mark which are true or false. Your answers are unique to you, not right nor wrong. They provide you a chance to make your voice known. They are conversation starters. As your board compares its answers, we trust clear choices for growth together will be made obvious. In this chapter we discuss identity.

THE FIVE MUST-HAVE CONVERSATIONS ABOUT IDENTITY

IDENTITY | TRUE / FALSE

Identity | Distinct blend of characteristics expressing the self.

- We reaffirm our origin story.
- We make values mentionable.
- We align our walk with our talk.
- We honor stakeholders' identities, while true to ours.
- We make time to hear our members' stories.

CulturallyConsciousBoard.com

THE BOARD PLACEMAT

1. **We reaffirm our origin story.** How often does your board review why it was founded and what values shaped it in the past and in its current state? Does your board orientation include these elements? What are the marks of heroes your organization celebrates? Which features of your origin story must stakeholders be reminded of? Are there harms or hurts in your organization's history that need to be owned or aired with its stakeholders?

2. **We make values mentionable.** Values are boundaries, guardrails that free us to be clear about our shared aspirations. When nearing or overstepping boundaries, does your board cultivate a permission-giving environment that allows members to speak freely or provides opportunities for feedback? Who does your board turn to during hard conversations? When forces beyond the table exert pressure to change your values-informed approach, what internal disciplines does your board rely on to guide group decision-making? (CONTINUED)

3. **We align our walk with our talk.** Just as Hope International had to confront dilemmas between identity-keeping and donor dependence, even at risk of loss of resources for vulnerable stakeholders, what mission-centered dilemmas must your board discuss? How does your board connect mission to its outcomes? Recognizing how risk can reveal a "fight, flight or freeze" mode that brings other cultural factors to the table, does your board take time for scenario planning? What is a recent opportunity your board was presented with, and how did you navigate your decision-making? What tools did you use?

4. **We honor stakeholders' identities, while remaining true to ours.** Reputation is the collective judgment of your stakeholders. What mechanisms allow you to hear your various stakeholders? What current board habits encourage or discourage participative leadership? Does your board educate itself about its stakeholders? Does the board invite DEI perspectives and training? Do you discourage and address insensitive attitudes or conduct? If so, how? How has it strengthened your board culture? Where are there gaps?

5. **We make time to hear board members' personal stories.** Agendas are full of much-needed tasks. Recognizing that knowing one another is an asset in times of crisis, does your board prioritize times to hear one another's journeys? What ritual might you weave into your meetings to allow for this?

8

Intention

At crucial moments of choice,
most of the business of choosing is already over.

IRIS MURDOCH[35]

Phil relished getting to the board meetings an hour before everyone else. He had a ritual: He opened the storage room, where the antique table he had donated to City Farm was kept and protected. He pulled out the table, polished it lightly, arranged the chairs appropriately and reflected. He opened the drawers of the table, where etched on the wooden plank, underneath the assortment of notepads, agendas and pens, were the initials B. P. W.—Bruno Phil Wagner—his grandfather and namesake, although he just went by Phil. He remembered sitting on Grandfather's lap, at this very same table, as he'd sketch portraits. Bruno was a farmer because that was the vocation offered to him during the Depression. But his true love was art, a passion he kept close to his vest, except when with his grandson. Phil was probably only three or four, so it wasn't the specifics of the memory, but the feelings and even aroma that he retained. A feeling of safety, pride, combined with the smell of freshly mowed hay.

His grandfather came to the United States from Germany as a toddler in 1907. His family were the "undesirables" of their time. They moved to Chicago, then Cincinnati, and finally settled in the Niagara Falls area of Buffalo. The older his grandfather got, the more he would revert to his childhood German, whispering *mein Kind* to his grandson. Phil would hold on to those words as long as he could before his own father would yell, "Use English, Dad. Use English."

Phil knew he was an American. No hyphens here. His grandfather told him how President Wilson said of German Americans that "any man who carries a hyphen about with him, carries a dagger that he is ready to plunge into the vitals of this Republic when he gets ready."[36] The message was loud and clear. If they didn't assimilate, his family didn't belong. It irritated him now, with everyone hyphenating and using acronyms to identify themselves. For him, it was a sign of oppression, a tearing at the republic his grandfather had fought so hard to be a part of. Because for all its flaws, America was still the land of opportunity. His grandparents and parents found economic success, through hard work. When World War II came, wanting to prove his patriotism, his grandfather tried to enlist. But a back injury prevented his enlistment. He wanted that for the next generation though.

Phil's father served in Korea. After a knee injury blew Phil's chances of being in the NFL, he continued both their legacies, serving with distinction in Vietnam. But he never forgot being spat on when he returned. "I fought for your right to spit on me," he used to say to the shaggy-haired hippies who were crawling all over upstate New York at the time, at least after Woodstock. As he got older and learned about the Pentagon's reasons for the war, he began to empathize. He did what he could to mend the past, and tonight he was still trying to help.

Phil first came across City Farm while working on one of his commercial real estate deals. His grandfather had always worked land that belonged to others, at least until he was much older. He saved enough to buy his own parcel. When opportunities arose, he purchased and annexed nearby family farms. By the time he passed away, he owned one of the most productive agricultural farms in upstate New York.

Phil had learned through listening to those stories that owning capital is everything. He was determined to never suffer like his grandparents and parents had. And here he was, a respected commercial real estate developer. He always went with the surveyors to get a feel for each property he bought and developed. When he was given the chance to turn the old Boys & Girls Club building into a multipurpose office complex in Baker Park, he jumped at the chance. He could see the profits coming in. And then he met Sierra. She was one of the protestors of the new building. He had PTSD from the Vietnam War protests and could feel the anger rising in him. It took one step of faith from Sierra, to put down her sign and reach out her hand. "Mr. Wagner, I'm Sierra. I wonder if we could just grab coffee. No press. No recordings. I just want to hear your vision for this property."

Before he knew it, he and his vice president, Mary, were meeting every other week with Sierra. They came to understand her concern for the citizens of Baker Park. She heard his heart for economic opportunity. And together they worked to make a plan that would work for everyone. It wasn't without its tensions, but before they knew it, a mixed commercial-residential coflourish was formed. To honor his grandfather, Phil worked with Sierra to create a minifarm in the middle of the community. City Farm was his pride and joy. A way to tap back into his roots. And he was proud of the board they had built. He liked things the way they were, and his entrepreneurial mind couldn't stop spinning with ideas to transform not just City Farm, but the entire community. Sometimes he couldn't separate those.

And so these new board members coming on, questioning his authority, really unnerved him. It was as if they didn't appreciate all that had taken place to get City Farm to where it was today. And so he'd come back to that table at the start of each meeting, almost trying to receive wisdom from the past to help him today.

Visible Alignment

Your board is solid in its identity. It knows who it is. Now, it needs to have the capacity to align its aspirations with practical outcomes. Leaving such an important promise, implied by your mission, to the whimsy of a flawed, unexamined fulfillment system could border on fiduciary malpractice. As it's been said, "If your visibility outpaces your capability, you soon will lose your credibility."[37] In other words, a process is the only thing standing between your organization's best intentions and its actual impact. Your capacity must be completely aligned to ensure your aspirational talk matches with strategy results talk. Show the world you have an organizational walk—a reliable process—and they will bring the whole world with them. That is what happened to a friend of ours, Ron.

Before retirement, Ron was a food industries executive. He knew how to get the food from the farms and freezers to restaurants, schools and institutions of all kinds—to the people, writ large. In his spare time, he was a volunteer, joining the board of Meals on Wheels People of

Portland. For 12 years, he fed through governance. But passion is sticky, continuing well after the board is adjourned. So, he took a delivery route, "Tigard #18," he smiles. Caring can snowball. Ron talked up his route at work. He told of Miss Caroline (who kept a Polaroid camera and a sharpie, to remember each name of the people who brought food and stayed awhile). Eighteen of his staff joined the feeding frenzy. He told of lasting friendships made during cooler pickups. While the pandemic tested many organizations, Meals on Wheels People of Portland never missed a delivery. Why? Ron was only one volunteer. But the snowball was 1,500 Rons, and at no additional cost. Volunteers were the capital. Their cause—food and a friend—ensured outcomes matched intentions.

When intentions have the outcomes in mind, the impacts are powerful. We offer a cautionary tale of what happens when they do not.

The Best of Intentions

Roger (not his real name) is an East African entrepreneur who empowers entire communities to be self-sustaining. Tired of waiting for others to solve problems for his community, he encouraged a transformed mindset as a way to lift themselves out of poverty. His approach has launched hundreds of businesses, transforming thousands of lives.

One of his projects was situated in a very rural community. Locals assessed their assets and started a bakery. It grew and employed many. Their largest buyer was a school across the hill, run by another nonprofit organization with similar good intentions. With an influx of high-net-worth donors, they transformed the school into the best physical structure in the region. Donor intent shaped decision-making for the organization. The government was all smiles when hosting these wealthy guests. But word on the street was: when the wealthy donors tired of the school in a few years, the government would eagerly assume control.

While Roger's bakery project had been operating in the community for a long time, the new organization decided to start baking their own bread, without conversation with their neighbor. Before Roger knew it, the donor-funded nonprofit built a professional kitchen, shutting down his village's economy. There was never a conversation about partnership. The good intentions of one organization squashed the dreams of the village next door.

We can assume the board of the wealthier organization had the best intentions. But what were the hidden, unspoken cultural perceptions that prevented them from consulting their neighbors and the local economic balance? What biases or trust-breaking mindsets may have been at play in this scenario? This chapter urges boards to reconsider their most recurrent questions: to spend or not spend and to reflect on how those decisions reveal a board's cultural priorities. While not everything can be anticipated, this does not excuse fiduciary officers from failing to interrogate all that is within their conscious grasp. Practicing a methodical humility based on what can be known through such tools as SWOT, Scenario Planning or PESTLE Analyses—Political, Economic, Sociocultural, Technical, Legal and Environmentally (each learnable through web searches), invites stakeholders to be relieved of investment blindfolds. This is where a culturally conscious board can truly shine.

Talking Through Intention Using the Placemat

We have fashioned several statements followed by conversation starter questions related to intention. Do these statements describe your board? If the statement describes your board, mark it as true in the text or on the placemat. Mark it as false if the statement does not. What do you notice about the statements, especially in light of this chapter?

THE FIVE MUST-HAVE CONVERSATIONS ABOUT INTENTION

INTENTION | TRUE / FALSE

Definition | Having a purpose or goal, designing for a specified future, proceeding on a course.

- We consult mission, vision, values during decisions.
- We examine policies for fairness, equity and inclusion.
- We expect status reports on the mission-based promise to stakeholders.
- We are convinced our theory of change makes a difference.
- We orchestrate our progress through a strategic plan.

CulturallyConsciousBoard.com

THE BOARD PLACEMAT

1. **We consult mission, vision and values during decisions.** Having read that your audience is only your audience to the degree your identity matters to theirs, is it obvious why your board might want to put this on the table? Does anyone bring up the mission in your boardroom? Is it written on the agenda? Do your board members, staff and volunteers know it? Does anyone yet have it memorized? Should they?

2. **We examine policies for fairness, equity and inclusion.** In the social media–saturated ecosystem in which your organization seeks to influence and is simultaneously thereby influenced, does it make sense to live in consultation with board peers on how your board and other mission participants show up in matters of fairness, equity or inclusion? Has there been an analysis of fair employment practices, such as equal pay? Who has been hired, fired and promoted within the organization?

3. **We expect status reports on the mission-based promise to stakeholders.** Given our assumption that the organization's

(CONTINUED)

promise is not the purview of marketing or development staff, but that of the board, why might "status reports" on the progress of the mission be indicative of a culturally conscious board? If progress reports are expected, is everyone clear about what must be measured and why? Is anyone prepared to put on the table what they need and do not need, what they consider critical and irrelevant to their tracking and reporting practices? Given the governance and operational separation, what does the board need to know in order to generate both policy guidance and routine oversight?

4. **We are convinced our theory of change makes a difference.** Are you convinced the way your organization delivers its promise creates change? Whose voices do you hear when assessing it? Could you draw your theory of change on a napkin, explain how it creates change in a step-by-step manner? Does your board think you should be able to? Has it equipped you to do so? Would your staff or stakeholders expect this degree of technical knowledge about the promise fulfillment system?

5. **We orchestrate our progress through a strategic plan.** If this is not true of your organization, how do you and the staff account for the action being funded year after year? Do you take time to look back, to celebrate the turning-point moments that signaled your organization was making gains in its mission, visibility, capacity building or report card items? Has your market changed and, if so, is your board set up to understand the new strategic landscape? Would a unified set of assumptions about where you are, where you are going, what you need and the critical path to get there impact your organization's credibility, visibility or capacity?

9

Invitation

When any key member of an emotional system can control their own emotional reactiveness and accurately observe the functioning of the system and their part in it and they can avoid counterattacking when provoked and when they can maintain an active relationship with the other key members without withdrawing or becoming silent, the entire system will change in predictable ways.

MURRAY BOWEN, M.D.[38]

The words were clear. They were right there, printed in black and white. And the meaning was immediately clear. "Next time, get a woman." The secretary for that meeting was certainly terse in the summary of the discussion. Looking at the top of the page, Crystal could see that the crumpled sheet she had found, in the side drawer of *the* board table, was dated three months before her first board meeting.

Her labored thought: "Guess they 'got' me?" Crystal smiled peevishly; she wondered what must have been the story that night when several men told themselves, and then seriously deliberated about, and finally concluded something that ended up in the minutes as, literally, "Next time, get a woman." What problem must a woman (namely *she* as that selfsame woman) solve for the group that deliberated that evening?

While this may have been Crystal's first time around as a board member, it wasn't her first time being a woman on a mostly male work team. Neither was it her first time being the youngest in a small group. Crystal knew this position like the back of her hand, the ins and outs of its contours. She had made peace with the structure of reality that lived in the minds of unchallenged colleagues. They did not know it when they asked her, but she knew it when she answered: her participation obligated her to care, not just for "their target audience," but for every one of these new colleagues and friends. She also knew, this was going to come with a cost.

Michael's years of moving in and out of varied cultures gave him an intuitive read on body language. He could see the tension in Crystal's face, the crumpled paper in her hand. He recognized the script and remembered reading the minutes from that meeting months ago, thinking they didn't accurately summarize their conversation. But, they were just minutes, so they got the gist, and he'd let it go this time.

It really began with a mistake. Sierra had invited a sixth board member to serve—a respected public relations executive. She and Phil thought he would be a great addition. They added a chair to their boardroom table, but he didn't show. Her phone rang and it was the new member, apologizing that a media crisis for a local company required his assistance. He'd make it the next time. The next time came and another crisis pulled him away. Sierra made an excuse that "it was okay" because his clout alone would be helpful to their fundraising.

In that moment, Michael realized they had an opportunity. He wrote down, "Next time, get a woman" and then stopped without writing the rest of his thought and said out loud, "Do you see that chair? It's sat empty for two months now, and I think it is an invitation for us to think about who we are as a board and what voice is truly missing from the table that can help us accomplish our mission in this time of growth. To be honest, outside of my own journey, no one else on this board is from this neighborhood in recent years. And I've sensed a paternalism in many of our recent decisions that needs to be named. I fear, even in myself, that we view the people we are serving as the 'other' who are in dire need of our help, rather than us recognizing we need their voice. This new board member may be super busy, but his commitment rings hollow by the lack of his presence.

"You know, it was my mom who was the one who carried the weight for our family when we lived here. Most of the refugees working in the garden are women. Jemma will be signing off the board soon because of her health, and she hasn't been able to attend most of the meetings. The female refugees open up to Sierra, but not to us. I know we need marketing / public relations experience, but I also feel like we need the voice of either a refugee or someone who understands this context."

And so the chair sat empty.

Until Crystal arrived.

Crystal now looked like she was going to say something, and Michael quickly interjected, "You know, Crystal, a few months ago we asked ourselves whose voice was needed at this table for this particular moment in our organization's history. We recognized some blind spots we've had, and your voice is exactly what we needed to fulfill our mission. But we've not truly taken the time to hear from you about what brought you here. If

> you're comfortable, or we can do it at the next meeting, would
> you share with us what has drawn you to this mission? In fact,
> it would be good for all of us to remind ourselves why we were
> invited to this table and why we stay."
>
> Crystal looked at him from that chair. It was no longer empty.

An Empty Chair Is Always Speaking

What your board does with an empty chair is a big deal. Imagine the
organization you serve. Who sits around the table? Who makes the
decisions? You do not need an expensive workplace climate audit to
figure out not only who is missing, but who is taking up all the available air. Whose perspective would deepen your capacity to fulfill your
mission more completely? This can be in expertise, gender, race, ethnicity or age. A board growing in its cultural consciousness has begun
a journey acknowledging that the quality and comprehensiveness of
its decisions are limited by its perspective. It allows for some shuffling
of seats or rearrangement of furniture so that the greater good can
flourish. Doing this is an act of hospitality.

Hosts and Guests: The Leader's Continual Pivot

You are the newest member of a historically large foundation in a small
but growing city, backing over 125 small nonprofits. Funding has tradi-
tionally been granted through an informal "old boys' network" where
friends of friends could expect a high likelihood of a grant request's
success. The network is the same, but the community has changed.
New factories are drawing immigrants from Mexico and Central
America, who now make up 60% of a previously Eastern European
population, but nearly a quarter of families live below the poverty line.

The board is composed of male business leaders from the community, who are nearing retirement age. In the last 10 years, only two women have joined the board. You notice that a few innovative projects aiding service workers' English education and providing car repairs for low-income families consistently face rejection with little discussion. You have suggested the board diversify, especially with its aging members, but the chair continues to push back saying that "diversity divides." He is concerned about losing the foundation's values (and supporters!). You are concerned about the true impact of the foundation's grants on the community. In this real-life scenario, what is on and what is off the table? How does a culturally conscious board decide?

It is difficult to fake the disposition of a host. Either you are credible as the kind of person who says *mi casa, su casa* (and means it) or you are not. If you are, you live in such a way that guests decide the authenticity of your welcome. Should they come, they will find you ready. To greet those who would enjoy your care and provisions is as much a delight for you as you intend it to be for them.

Leaders with the most lasting appeal often share similarities with the best hosts, the world over, at least in the opinions of those who are made to feel visible by their welcome and attention. When leaders bring this gracious mindset to their board efforts, they contribute to an atmosphere of warmth, inclusivity and collaboration. Their capacity to withstand the necessary tensions that inevitably arise when families, friends and social circles encounter trust-defining moments of truth will almost always cost them something.

But nothing awakens awareness like conflict. Few emotions are as difficult to navigate as those that arise when we are being misunderstood, reduced to the size of a box that is way too small for our identity and intentions. What we do in moments like these, especially if we are yet in the low social capital trust-building phase, can define the trajectories of personal, organizational and real lasting histories. The

Murray Bowen quote that begins this chapter bears emphasizing: if such a leader can withstand these tensions "without withdrawing or becoming silent, the entire system will change in predictable ways." An invitation to the table is also an invitation to remain at the table when the work gets hard, when it would be easier to move faster in isolation.

We take a closer look at the notion of a guest-and-host pivot through a story that was shared with us. As we do, keep in mind that a culturally conscious board and board members who embody the promise of this outcome are people on a journey of accumulated learning, sorting out the maturing role of community and belonging in their lives.

The story unfolds in one of the most diverse zip codes in the United States. The board of a multiethnic faith community prided itself on its diverse constituency. More than 100 years old, this community stayed put when so many churches in the 1970s fled the city centers. With a storied legacy of welcome as old as its protest of segregated pews for Blacks and whites during the Civil War, this community practiced a kind of cultural consciousness that kept its doors open to new-arrival refugees from Laos, Cambodia, Thailand and Vietnam. It was intentional in how it invited displaced people. And it was intentional in seeking to have diverse voices on its board. Yet, it is difficult to both welcome a newcomer and insist that the newcomer is only a guest. Perhaps you have heard people say "First visit, you are a guest; next visit, get your own lemonade from the fridge." Guests eventually take their seats.

When we have been newcomers, especially when we have been perceived to hold less power or social standing (but perhaps more experience in what is *not* fully on the table), we secretly have wanted to know, How much of me do you really want? Do I have to "go along to get along" with "your way or the highway"? Few are likely to ask the questions surrounding unequal power, especially if they have unequal power, regardless of their socioethnic makeup: "When in Rome, do as the Romans" remains the prevailing advice when you are in the one-down position, when you are "the stranger." Conformity is a survival strategy.

In this story, there were rumblings from the community about how decisions were really being made. The leader forced an uncomfortable conversation on a divided board. He put the matter on the table by requiring all board members to read a book together. All would be invited to respond. That is where things got a bit messy.

One board member read the book studiously. True to his lived experience, informed as a financial analyst with two master's degrees and lived experience as an Army Ranger, he wrote out a point-by-point summary that allowed him to get his thoughts on paper, shifting perspectives. He drew conclusions after thoughtful analysis. Soldiers are sticklers for knowing and completing their mission. And then he emailed his thoughts to the other board members.

Another board member approached the same task in an entirely different way. She read the book too; that was the board assignment. She could not boast of degrees, but her reputation was worth gold in this zip code. Her family had lived in this neighborhood for decades. Her community transformed dispute and differences with "living words" not "frozen"[39] like those in tightly knit essays. In times of trouble, they sat down together for coffee at the local diner.

She assumed the board would read and then discuss the book at the next board meeting. But something about the first board member's preemptive email rubbed her the wrong way. She accused him of using his education and the lengthy email as forms of racism and privilege. She protested the use of the written word to stifle authentic conversation. One assignment (on the table), two approaches (usually, off the table), uncomfortable board table conflict now out and on the table. He went on the defensive. She went on the defensive. They were at a stalemate and board tensions were high.

We pause here for a brief digression before we finish the story. Some of the invitations we make unmask hidden biases, make us uncomfortably aware of how *our way*—sometimes personal, sometime cultural—could easily fall short in the eyes of others. The culturally conscious board takes seriously the liabilities that attend a single point of view. It is practiced in surfacing those cultural stress points, to evaluate how bias is at work in ourselves first (if we happen to have the presence to hesitate and entertain whether others' attributions might justifiably appear to be true to them). *This* is when the pivot between host and guest matters. That said, we continue with our story.

The first board member in this story represented a way of hosting decision-making processes by which the congregation had predominantly functioned for most of its 100 years. Written documents. Formal language. His intentions were honorable and he knew them. Intimidation was not his way. His education, experience and sense of duty were how he always put skin in the game when he cared about something. These attributes lay in the background for him. Yet, he recognized pain when he saw it. Something happened. Whatever it was that brought about such an alarming accusation, he had to get past the sting, recover something of his better presence and let curiosity lead the way. To get it, really get it, he would have to welcome a shift within himself, a perspective shift (or, as we prefer to call it, *a culture shift*).

They were both serving the same mission, yet she described feeling as though she were a stranger to her own neighborhood. Her voice was not truly invited to the table. He asked if they could meet. So she suggested the diner. He went there just to listen. She was able to protest the assumption of what was the right form to use to resolve the community dispute; she shared how rational argumentation, a seldom-questioned cultural artifact tied to literacy's role in technological power, divides. She was able to voice a different way, one that was as old as her ancestors.

As he had done with his email, she became the host in *that* setting. They both pivoted. Both sought to take the perspective of the other. It didn't happen overnight. It took months of hard conversations between them and the rest of the board. There were times when some wanted to leave the table; ultimately, they all chose to remain. When we make room for humility, trust rises among those committed to a mission greater than themselves. As board members prioritized connection, changes in key areas of programming began taking place. The tokenism many felt was replaced by active participation. The mission did not change. There were still guiding parameters, but the systems and structures began to shift as their perspectives shifted.

Each of their pivots takes us back to cultural humility as a catalyst for trust. Our boards, like our communities, are situated increasingly in cultural spaces antagonized by extreme ideologies. Polarization is the norm in an era of outrage and cultural wedge issues, designed by professional political strategists and advertising-dollar-driven news outlets. Many do not trust those with whom they disagree. But boards govern in this unhelpful context; in fact, boards must consciously lead. Deliberative bodies and what they do in the social-impact and nonprofit sectors make a difference at the most local of levels. And in terms of how they bring unity and cohesion, they can become one of the mending places in our frayed social fabric.

Talking Through Invitation Using the Placemat

We have fashioned several statements followed by conversation questions related to invitation to help identify moments of truth that test the depth of welcome with your stakeholders. Review each. Mark it as true if the statement describes your board. Mark it as false if the statement does not describe your board. No matter whether the statement is true or false, the conversation it provokes is the purposeful work.

THE FIVE MUST-HAVE CONVERSATIONS ABOUT INVITATION

INVITATION | TRUE / FALSE

Definition | Welcoming participation, politely increasing chances, offering incentive.

- We leverage our mission and story to attract stakeholders.
- We recruit members who add capacity, not merely fit.
- We glean stakeholder feedback to lift our cultural blindfolds.
- We embody a partnership of equals, a participatory approach.
- We cultivate diverse candidate pools when recruiting.

CulturallyConsciousBoard.com

THE BOARD PLACEMAT

1. **We leverage our mission and story to attract stakeholders.** Your organization has a reason for being. A founding story inspires. Who are the various stakeholders in your organization? When you consider diversifying your outreach, how do you partner with your beneficiaries to attract more stakeholders? How has your board utilized advisory boards to expand its network?

2. **We recruit members who add capacity, not merely fit.** To ensure an excellent board that increases your impact, you want to add capacity. What is the current makeup of the board and leadership team? What voice is missing? Is there an area of expertise that is lacking? Is there an intentional recruitment effort being made to diversify the team? Do board members come in one at a time, or is there opportunity to recruit a cohort?

3. **We glean stakeholder feedback to lift our cultural blindfolds.** Feedback is vital to ensuring that what is off the table is

(CONTINUED)

put on the table. Is the voice of your beneficiaries represented at the boardroom table? Where do you recognize implicit biases during your board meetings? Or not? How does your board cultivate growth in areas of weakness or blind spots? Are there requirements for being on the board that may prohibit more diverse perspectives?

4. **We embody a partnership of equals, a participatory approach.** A say-anything culture requires deep trust. What cultural practices might encourage or prevent participative leadership? How is the executive session used to ensure everyone has an opportunity to use their voice?

5. **We cultivate diverse candidate pools when recruiting.** If you were to take an honest look at your board recruitment matrix, where are there gaps? You may live in an area that may be very homogeneous. How do you understand "diverse" candidate pools? What voices are missing from the table?

Visit culturallyconsciousboard.com for practical tools on recruitment, onboarding, advisory board development, term limits and cohort development, please .

10

Investment

Risk is an essential need of the soul. The absence of risk produces a kind of boredom which paralyses in a different way from fear, but almost as much.

SIMONE WEIL[40]

Crystal's lips tightened, a habit she had developed as a child when she knew she had to "hold her tongue" when she disagreed with adults. The board packet had arrived two hours before tonight's meeting—again. She would have to request (again) that the chair send out board packets at least a week before meetings, two if possible. But that was the least of her concerns for the upcoming session. Things had improved since that last exchange with Michael. The last business item on the lengthy agenda simply read "Report: Buffalo City Planners Approve Land Offer/Purchase for $1." Phil's name was listed next to the agenda item.

Crystal had already made her concerns known six months ago about the expansion to a second site in downtown Buffalo, especially with the stipulations that required City Farm to create a homeless shelter as part of their occupancy use charter. Naturally, she was not opposed to finding solutions to houselessness. She simply urged the board to consider whether this was City Farm's mission. Michael had questioned, "How do we pay for the care and feeding of the building after its purchase... that's not going to be $1." Phil had assured both at the time, "We would not be considering this generous offer from the city if it wasn't in our best interest." Since the item had only been a report by Phil at the time, of something that might develop, and no formal action had been taken by the board, both Crystal and Michael had let the matter rest that evening.

That was months ago. But now, here it was on the agenda tonight. Had Phil gone ahead and talked to city planners without a green light from the board? She looked at her watch—less than an hour to grab a bite and get to the meeting before Phil's gavel ("that hammer," she called it under her breath) came slamming down.

"If you'll just calm down, Crystal," Phil urged.

"Oh *no*, he didn't just 'If you'll just calm down, missy' *me*"—the words were still reverberating in her hot eardrums. Crystal *hated* to be told to "calm down." She hated it doubly when she was calm already. She was speaking when he interrupted her. That's how she knew she was still in control. But now, he was standing up and flashing both hands as if counting to 50 by 10s and bidding her "calm down." Wasn't he aware of the real storm that brews behind the thinning, blinking eyelids of a kid who knew what followed if someone tried to muzzle her point of view? Phil had picked the wrong night to go parental on her.

As he continued to mansplain the merits of the deal and what so-and-so said and to whom, Crystal retreated internally to have a meeting with both her tongue and her temper. She simply whispered, "Only one of you two can be held in the next few minutes. Tongue, you had better go first, because he doesn't even want to have a face-to-face meeting with Crystal who really *needs* to be calmed down, even though he came quite close to seeing it."

When Crystal spoke next, it was in a deliberate, half-paced tone that seemed to clap heavily, like car doors being shut, with each word. "Phil. I. am. calm. But, I should not be. Nor should anyone else in this room be calm. You have acted independently of this board's consent, violating the tentative agreements to table the building donation until we were satisfied this was the right choice for City Farm. But you have been acting independently, with no authority to do so. Calm down? I am calm. But I am also curious. I am curious about what you deem is the role board members are to play in decision-making.

"I think the city's offer is generous, and I also think we cannot afford to accept it at this time under these stated conditions. I do not see you have proffered an affordability or workable use plan. The staff appear confused by meetings you had with some of them lately (which we knew nothing about). You are inviting me to calm down. Okay, please help me understand why this is okay for you to do? Can I just go out and bind the corporation into a capital maintenance plan, without board deliberation, consent, budget clearance or a strategy? You have drinks with a National Guard buddy, and now we are obligated to generate an added $980,000 by this time next year and every year after that? Your plan does not reflect the true cost of business. But most importantly, Phil, I have been waiting for you to say it, but you haven't. This is not our mission. The city's generous offer is for a different kind of organization. We are not a homeless shelter. And I do not know why you don't know that." Crystal reached for her latte and took a slow, steady sip, cautious not to end up with a frothy mustache after this dramatic speech.

Phil stared back in apparent disbelief at having been addressed in this way. This didn't work for his senior/junior chain-of-command brain. So, to awaken him to the conversation of equals she believed herself to be in at the moment, she added: "I'm certainly ready to listen."

Hearing her own voice speaking again, she truly knew she was indeed calm. But she was more than calm, she was vested.

Spend, Don't Spend?

When economic development organizations planted thousands of moringa trees decades ago, they did not work closely with the farmers to develop the supply chain. The result was broken promises to several thousand farmers, and fields of dormant trees. A company recognized the lost potential and worked hard to restore broken trust with farmers and lay out a new vision of what could be. However, the farmers needed to see immediate benefit to their families before they were willing to try replenishing their fields. Over the next seven years, deep relational connections were forged between the Rwandan manager and the farmers. Trust was restored and earned. Foreign investors were willing to delay immediate returns on investment for the greater good.

Then COVID-19 hit. New sales with leading international cosmetic companies, which used moringa oil, were on hold because of the inability to ship across the Atlantic. Emergency funds were established for the farmers, but after several months the board had a hard choice to make. Its immediate stakeholders were the farmers, whose livelihoods depended on this income. The question before the board was: "Are we a social impact business or a charity? These funds are creating dependencies. If we are an actual business and we want this to thrive for 10 years, not just 1 year, then we may need to lay off workers and tell the farmers to wait another year for sales to be restored. What is the right thing to do?"

In the end, the board of advisors recognized their mission was to be a social impact business and that that would guide their decision-making. In this case, after listening to various stakeholders, from farmers in the fields to the CEO of a billion-dollar company, they sorted through the trade-offs and made the very difficult decision to lay off some workers. It was a short-term hit with the belief that their prospects would turn around once the supply chain and shipping routes were reestablished. The decision created much dismay, but within a year they were able to rehire the workers and are now profitable. Go into any Body Shop in the United States and you will see their products beautifully displayed. Intentionality paid off.

Conscious Investment:
Culture's Paradox in Transformation

Every organism exists in the tension of two unceasing pursuits. One impulse is to *stabilize*. The other is to *sustain*. Robert Terry links internal dispositions toward scarcity and plenty with the decision-maker's stances toward stability and chaos.[41] At one end of this spectrum, stability impulses require certainty, consistency, compliance, order, closure, unity. The structures, policies and values at this end of the spectrum ensure the world is a steady, undisturbed base of operations. This world is predictable, even comfortable. Status quo can masquerade as stability. This is pictured in Figure 10.1, Culture's Ceaseless Twin Pursuits.

At the other end, sustainability impulses require growth, viability and innovation. We sense that a transforming vision of the future comes with inherent costs. Usually, the weightier the change, the heftier the necessary investment. (Status quo has already been funded after all.) It's familiar. But innovation and transition to a new order,

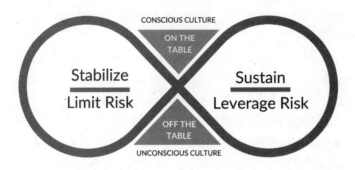

FIGURE 10.1 Culture's Ceaseless Twin Pursuits

especially the kinds for which nonprofits often exist, require courageous investments of time, talent, treasure and technique.

Shortly after Jennifer's family first moved to the Beacon Hill neighborhood of Seattle, they invited all the neighbors over for an open
house. Only two neighbors—who looked a lot like them—showed up.
While they got to know one another, complaints surfaced about unsupervised kids loitering at the adjacent gas station.

Fast-forward three years. Her family offered another open house,
but this time as a BBQ for those neighborhood kids. They did the same
as they had that first month—handed out invitations. But something
different happened. Six kids came to that first BBQ. Within months,
four dozen were attending regularly. What made the difference? Perhaps word spread about the free burgers, outdoor billiards and movies
screened on the side of their house. But it was more than that. It was
the three years of investing in friendships with those "unsupervised
kids" at the gas station. Jennifer's family and neighbors enjoyed one-
off conversations, called neighbors by their names when they walked
by, joined sidewalk marbles games, offered practical help to families
when invited. This time they were known and trusted.

Admittedly, although these events were well intended, they had
not planned for every eventuality. In fact, they were robbed. First,

Jennifer's wallet, then the video camera and finally their trust. Although the intent to be hospitable was not responsible for the broken trust, that intent measured any sentimental notion of what it means to be good neighbors. Trust, especially when shaken, comes with costs. Trust required conscious design: forgiveness, ground rules and boundaries. It required conscious investment: time, money and trust, but not as they initially thought of investment. As they stepped into the worlds of these kids—a mixture of straight-A students, gang members, prostitutes—they paid the intangible costs of releasing power attached to the money, structure and even who starred in the roles of hosts or guests. The kids led the conversations, helped flip burgers and hosted games. Transformation was reciprocal as each invested in the other. Deeper trust was the new return on investment, an investment of values.

Return on Values: Outcomes-Conscious Commitments

Budgets, by their mathematical nature, are not vague. In fact, they can be as inescapable as a mirror in what they reveal about what an organization really cares about. The assumptions and the people who designed the budget may be vague, but when a board approves a budget, it simultaneously reaffirms that these line items are in complete alignment with and in service to the aspirational framework that justifies the organization's charter. A well-funded budget, tied to the staff-led transformative fulfillment process, is one of the biggest predictors of strategy success and ultimately stakeholder satisfaction.

Change comes with a price tag, always. We propose *conscious investment* as a method for assessing that price tag. It is neither avoidant nor reckless. It is both stability focused and sustainability focused. It requires a board to interrogate its values. It watches over the inadvertent paternalistic power dynamics, creating resource dependencies and provider-to-recipient structured relationships that can be all-too-comfortable for providers, but disempowering, if not dignity-damning, for those so-labeled recipients.[13] It requires its members to make explicit their own worldviews during decisions on resources, need, waste and want.

A set of principles (balanced scorecard, multiple bottom lines) might allow a team to mention the cost implied in a decision but also the costs of not deciding at the same time. Perhaps this happens already, through the natural discussion phase of your voting process. If not, here are a few suggested discussion items to help bring the unmentionable aspects of investment to the table.

Trade-offs. There are relative investments. Decision-makers are always making trade-offs. Are people most important, sustainability, growth? Recognizing the tradeoffs involved with a decision will force the values conversation to the table.

Ownership. Investment decisions are comprehensive in that they are relevant for all your stakeholders—your beneficiaries, vendors, staff. Investment decisions impact everyone. Ultimately it is about authority—who gets to decide and at what level you get to make an investment. Does the office manager get to decide how many paper clips? Does the CEO get to set the strategic budget for the next five years? Or does the board make all decisions, some? Clear guidelines on authority are important.

Sunsets. Sometimes nonprofits seek sustainability when what they should really have are sunset clauses and a willingness to go away if they've met their mission/goals. Too many seek to stay alive without really assessing if they're still needed.

Speak-ups. Sometimes the most honorable action available to you when you are witnessing a bad decision unfold is to find the courage and clarity to hold up the mirrors of the board and organization's own words—its mission, vision, values, its mandates, its promises. Trusting the better nature of your colleagues, point out what you cannot reconcile. Express curiosity as to how others have come to peace. Ask explicitly which values matter, when and why.

The status quo's appearance of stability hardly compares with the costs associated with a transforming vision of the future. Afterall, the status quo has already been funded. It's familiar. But innovation, change and transition to a new order, especially of the type for which nonprofits often exist, require courageous and intentional investments of time, talent and treasure.

Talking Through Investment Using
the Board Culture Placemat

In answering these true or false statements, you are taking stock of your values-based spending, evidence-based change and appreciative funding mindset, your own vested interest and how wisdom, wealth and work are nurtured on your board.

THE FIVE MUST-HAVE CONVERSATIONS ABOUT INVESTMENT

INVESTMENT | TRUE / FALSE

Definition | Committing resources, earning a return, acting for future advantage, engaging emotionally.

- We require budget priorities to reflect mission intent.
- We fund evidence-based efforts-to-outcome strategies.
- We ask "How can we afford it (or afford not to)?" instead of "Can we afford it?"
- We model our mission engagement by participating financially.
- We build board capacity through cultural mentors and advisors.

CulturallyConsciousBoard.com

THE BOARD PLACEMAT

(CONTINUED)

1. **We require budget priorities to reflect missional intent.** There are risks, opportunities and donors who call for your dollar investment. By what process does your board decide what is "worth it" (worth the time, worth the effort, worth the money, worth cutting losses)? What fiduciary decision-making model is currently in place?

2. **We fund evidence-based efforts-to-outcome strategies.** In the conversation regarding what is an output versus outcome, how does your board not only assess, but put money behind measuring what relates to your outcomes? What are the organizational behaviors and outcomes that are measured, encouraged and rewarded?

3. **We ask *How* can we afford it (or afford not to)? *instead of* Can we afford it?** As you think through trade-offs, ownership, sunsets and speak-ups, which of these areas would you like to see your board strengthen? What part of the stabilize-and-sustain diagram in Figure 10.1 do your board conversations focus on for the majority of the time?

4. **We model our missional engagement by participating financially.** A board that has 100% member giving is the gold standard. How does your board encourage this?

5. **We build board capacity through cultural mentors and advisors.** What outcomes does the board desire from its work toward becoming a culturally conscious board? What projects around increasing diversity and cultural consciousness do you fund? How do you react to failure and setbacks? Are there consequences when goals are not reached?

11

Impact

When a flower doesn't bloom,

you fix the environment in which it grows,

not the flower.

ALEXANDER DEN HEIJER[43]

The room fell quiet. Sierra stared at Phil. Michael took a deep breath. He seemed to do a lot of that lately. Phil's hands pushed against the worn grain of the farm table, his chair receding from its formal position. He looked over at Crystal, but all he could see were memories of protestors spitting on him. *Get it together, Phil,* he told himself. *You are more professional than this. What on earth are you reacting to?* Calmly, he spoke. "There are a lot of agenda items we need to cover tonight. I wasn't prepared for this kind of pushback on this board. You and I discussed this ahead of time, Sierra, and as the chair I'm going to move we table this until...."

"Phil," Michael began. Why was it in moments of conflict that he often felt like that teenage boy, literally fleeing from bullets? He took another deep breath. There was too much at stake here to walk away. He could feel it in the air. If each of them left the table, someone might not come back. Crystal had voiced a concern that had been simmering under the table for quite some time. But it wasn't just what she voiced. It was what her questions over the last six months had revealed.

The board of City Farm had a particular way of doing business that they had grown accustomed to. Michael looked around at the table and found himself appreciating each person for what they brought to the table. And in many ways, Phil's efficiency and business sense had helped them expand and grow. He knew Phil's story, but no one else really did. He could see the frustration on Crystal's face and the confusion on the face of Sierra and others.

The table before them felt like a literal metaphor for their current crisis. He saw the neatly lined agendas and pencils at each place setting, reflecting the way things were always done. He recognized that the only reason each member was there was that they had been invited, as guests, to this table—but the table was Phil's, passed down from his grandfather. He owned the table. Michael respected him for his role, but it was as if the table were causing them to be unconscious of the cultural changes they needed to make. He couldn't just blame Phil. They had each accepted this way of doing business because, bottom line, they had the social capital with Phil to trust his business sense. And in the past that had worked.

But here was someone whose voice represented the actual community they were serving, and she was bringing them back to the mission. That's what they were all there to serve anyway, wasn't it? And to be honest, as an attorney, he was surprised at how easily he had acquiesced in Phil's securing this deal. How had he lost sight of his fiduciary role, especially the legal one, to make sure that they were setting the organization up for financial sustainability in such a way that the mission was honored? Was their own way of being, their culture, becoming a liability? He looked around the room and it was as if for the first time he was seeing each of them, the dignity of each at the forefront.

He remembered that first night moving back to the States. Well, it was moving back for his mom, but for him it was a new country. New smells. Hearing his second language, not his first. The frost of the air moving through his body. And he remembered the feeling of walking into their apartment in Baker Park. Everyone stopped and stared. They didn't fit with the usual cross section of new tenants. An elderly man, wearing a uniform in his wheelchair, took the first step. He reached out his hand and welcomed them. The strangers.

"Isn't that the promise we are making to our beneficiaries, Phil? The promise to fulfill our mission? Crystal is right. Not because you're wrong. But because she's seeing something we've forgotten to prioritize. You and I would never enter into a deal like this in our professional settings without truly understanding the budgetary constraints and, more importantly, how this strategic change will affect the very people we are serving through City Farm. We always pledged to do things differently. To launch new business ventures that would create opportunity. Of course, serving the homeless sounds wonderful, but is it our mission? But at a deeper level, what does Crystal's question reveal about our own decision-making?"

Phil knew he had a decision to make: did he stay at the table or leave?

Inspect What Your Board Expects

Anything can be crowned a victory as long as no one bothers to define success. As Russ learned as a young white-glove-wearing Marine Corps drill instructor for Officer Candidates, "you do not get what you expect; you get what you inspect." In the case of impact, we simply cannot be better than the measurements we keep. More importantly, when the cultural distinctiveness of both board *and* stakeholders hold the key to intent (the criteria for success) and impact (the confirmation of success), we have to reconsider what passes for success.

Year after year, boards and donors are treated to annual reports on "accomplishments for the year." Often, a summary infographic outlines "the results" from the agency's efforts, with scorecards highlighting notable by-products of the work, such as 13 affordable homes built, 900 preschoolers registered, 40% fewer single moms in local shelters or 1,474 new subscribers since the campaign was launched. These are examples of *outputs*, which may fill annual reports but don't guarantee alignment with intended goals or transformative change.

Outcomes, on the other hand, determine a project's worth for the common good. They ask if the promise for transformation has been kept through these activities. This is much harder to answer unless outputs are always interrogated by their connection to the achievement of outcomes. We can ask instead, Do the results we experience align with the intentions we set for ourselves, that our stakeholders expect from us? Is our promise fulfilled in the lives of those whom we care most about? Have we done our work in a manner equal to our standards?

Boards often leave the answer to these questions to the staff. This is as it should be, *if* the work is the *execution* of the strategy. The strategy's implementation resides with the operational team certainly. However, the strategy's origins, ownership and authority derive from the board,

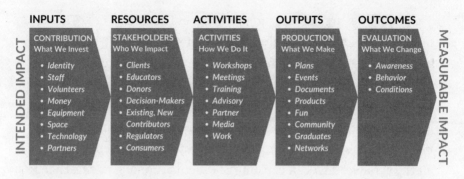

FIGURE 11.1 Logic Model, from Intention to Impact

not the executives or staff. The board's oversight function requires a growing intelligence that keeps pace with the impacts of the organization's efforts. The acceptability of results is within its jurisdiction. The board is the animating center of action founded upon the belief that what it authorizes and accounts for is also effectively generating transformative results in the actual world. (Figure 11.1)

The ABCs of Culturally Conscious Outcomes

Somewhere, someone in your organization really cares about your outcomes. We mean *really* cares. Most everyone knows who that is. They are in it for the right reasons. They can get quite serious, even insistent, about getting the service impact where it needs to be. They think about quality from the view of outsiders who cannot control the shape and adequacy of the outputs. They dutifully generate or review all the reports asked of them, even as they question whether the organization is measuring the wrong things in the wrong ways. They listen most seriously to the folks who can control the least. They focus on the gaps. This person, and we hope there are many, stays at the table, working toward the change that brings a hard-to-name satisfaction.

Does anyone from your board come to mind? How do you know?

Those qualities are not measured in busyness nor lots of talk. They are measured in impact. Transformation is not a theory. It is measured in proverbial or actual *before and after* pictures. The situation was X. After the process was applied and completed, we checked and learned the situation is Y. Provided they measured the right thing the right way, the change from X to Y demonstrates that a change has taken place. Of course, elaborate research projects can be erected to isolate all the variables that can explain the exact nature of how this change occurred, but it's really because someone cared about the long game. With that in mind, this practical exercise helps you think through your outcomes. Memorable as the Outcome ABCs: *awareness, behavior* and *conditions.*

Awareness. Consider whether your mission, if successfully delivered as intended, shifts the awareness of the people it cares about. Be clear about whether the program delivery process upon which your organizational promise relies is adequate to the task.

Behavior. Consider whether your mission, if successfully delivered as intended, invites its participants to change how they act, the process through which they achieve their aims. Being as exacting as you can be, what does a *before and after* picture look like?

Conditions. Consider whether your mission, if successfully delivered as intended, moves people toward a change in their conditions.

Consider your mission, your theory of change and its fulfillment process, asking yourself, and board, which of the outcomes in Figure 11.2 best match your expectations and promise. For each, ensure that a measure and data-tracking process exists, with reporting checkpoints equal to the importance of your stakeholders.

Impact does not occur in a vacuum. Impact is a by-product of all a team has done through its intentions, invitations, investments and

Change in Awareness	Change in Behavior	Change in Conditions
• Agency	• Ability	• Belonging
• Aspirations	• Action	• Capacity
• Attitudes	• Advocating	• Control
• Awareness	• Behavior	• Economic
• Beliefs	• Contributions	• Environment
• Bias	• Deciding	• Equity
• Effects	• Habits	• Family
• Identity	• Inclusion	• Legal
• Influences	• Policies	• Livelihood
• Intentions	• Practice	• Location
• Interest	• Protest	• Ownership
• Knowledge	• Relationships	• Political
• Learning	• Serving	• Social
• Motivations	• Social Action	• Spiritual
• Opinions	Skills	• Status
• Values	• Waste	• Systems

FIGURE 11.2 The ABCs of Outcomes

strategy decisions (and this, at times, for better and for worse). We agree, not all impacts are equal. While the best of intentions should be lauded, the best of intentions may not always outweigh negative or unintended impacts. Transformational impact is observable, not theoretical. Before and after pictures that recognize change in awareness, behaviors and conditions, with an efforts-to-impact fulfillment system in between, are imperative for boards to attest to stakeholders their aspirations and intentions have been met.

Talking Through Impact
Using the Board Culture Placemat

The outcomes-based and fidelity-focused statements below address your board's impact.

IMPACT | TRUE / FALSE

Definition | Producing a result, force of impression left, lasting, durable outcome.

- We measure our efforts by evidence-based outcomes regularly.
- We avoid dependency and parental mindsets.
- We compare results to stated intentions, promises.
- We harvest learning after events, milestones, fails, wins.
- We recognize, celebrate, encourage efforts of the team.

CulturallyConsciousBoard.com

THE BOARD PLACEMAT

1. **We measure our efforts by evidence-based outcomes regularly.** Taking a glance again at the lists of outputs and outcomes in this chapter, for what outcomes is your organization working? How does your organization know the status of your direct impact?

2. **We avoid dependency and parental mindsets.** Recognizing the community or cause you serve, what are ways your board seeks to avoid enabling dependency or parental mindset where you think you know better than those you serve?

3. **We compare our results to stated intentions and promises.** How does your organization reconcile that evidence gap between what it intends and what it measures about its progress toward impact?

4. **We harvest learning after events, milestones, fails and wins.** Notice what your board celebrates and when. How does your board address or receive information regarding the fails, as well as the wins? What are the feedback loops in the strategic planning process, as well as in board meetings?

5. **We recognize, celebrate and encourage efforts of the team.** The impact of your mission is most readily felt by the people who serve on the board and work for the organization. How are people celebrated? How does the organization react to failure or setbacks? Are there consequences when goals are not reached?

Further exercises regarding strategy decision screens, output/ outcomes report card and others are available on our website at culturallyconsciousboard.com.

EPILOGUE
Transformed Boards, Transformed Communities

Crystal stared at Michael. He had really affirmed her. As she began resting in that, she then quickly bristled and shrugged it off. *Typical*, she thought. *Another white man thinking he needs to validate me, as if my words weren't enough.* She was about to expand on her comments to Phil, but something caught her. It was the way he was steadying himself at the table, running his fingers over those very same cracks she had noticed at her first meeting six months ago. She had seen them as gaps between her and other board members, but the look in his eyes suggested that was not how he saw them.

She remembered a brief conversation with Sierra during a coffee break. Something about Phil's grandfather and the table. There was a kindness to Sierra's remarks that had touched Crystal. She now found herself going through all those former board meetings. She remembered the cringe when Phil started the Pledge of Allegiance, but over the months she had become aware of his past military service. Some things made sense now. She could hear her grandmother's voice again: "Take the plank out of your own eye before you take the needle out of another's." Yet, she knew she was right about this decision.

Phil just kept running his hands over the cracks in that damn table. What was eating at him? He trusted Michael. Well, he trusted Michael on legal matters. He expected Michael and others to trust him on business decisions. Yet, truth be told, this line of questioning made him question his own motives. Michael was right. If this were any other deal, he would have done the numbers, spoken to all the stakeholders and obtained the information he needed, so why didn't he do that here? And could he admit to Crystal and the others that he was wrong?

Sierra began to shuffle papers. She knew Phil. While she was grateful for the role he played on the board, she had known him long enough to know that when his mind was made up, there was no going back. She honestly didn't know what the right thing was to do. She knew they needed space to expand, and this opportunity seemed too good to be true. Phil made it seem possible. And weren't they all about being entrepreneurial? Yet, Crystal was raising something that really didn't seem to be about the $1 building and its maintenance costs. She paused with her papers and looked around the room.

An unspoken conviction seemed to set in. What if the deeper question they were failing to face was not about the mainte- nance costs of the city's $1 gift building, but about their own culture as a board—a question about motives, agendas, will- power—the unspoken distrust that seemed to permeate?

Phil sat there silently. The cracks seemingly larger than he remembered. So much history. And then, as if out of the wood- work, he heard the whispering of his old First Sergeant in Vietnam. "Lieutenant," he would shout before dawn, "what's the mission?" In the first weeks of his tour of duty, that berating voice would cause panic and frustration. "Why should I know?" he would silently scream back. "I'm just following orders." "Lieutenant!" he would hear again, "everyone should know the mission. I want to know that you've got my back, just as I have yours. And the only way to do that is for us all to know where we're going and why. Do you understand, Lieutenant?" At first he didn't, but after that horrible day when they lost half of their platoon to enemy fire, and he was overwhelmed by the chaos, he realized that the only thing that brought clarity was to remember the mission—"take the bunker." And so he moved forward, saving dozens more lives as a result. "What's our bunker...or my bunker?" he barely whispered to himself.

Michael could see the wheels turning in Phil. Something was different. And then he heard Phil say, "You're right, Crystal. I have been so focused on the shiny new deal that I missed how my actions were affecting everyone else. A homeless shelter is wonderful, but why are they making *us* do that, and not another organization that actually has experience and success in this area? When we talked about expansion in our strategic plan, we talked about streamlining in order to expand, not taking on new financial burdens. This should have been a much larger conversation, an opportunity to get feedback from all our stakeholders." Phil paused, looking down once more at that table. "We use this table at every meeting because it was carved by a farmer, an immigrant, who came to this country to flee oppression. He didn't find the acceptance he thought he would, but with hard work he created a life that I've benefited from. I promised myself as a young man that if I ever made it big, I'd help other people make it big too. That's why I came here. Somewhere in all of that, I've forgotten I can't do that alone. There's so much more I have to learn."

This was not what Crystal was expecting. Something had shifted. And it wasn't just because of her. It was all of them, almost seeing each other for the first time.

And then it happened—Phil moved his hands from the table, that symbol of the past, to the gavel, but he didn't pound it. Instead he extended it forward. "It's time," he said. "We've not had term limits. We've really just kept moving along because City Farm requires so much in the day-to-day. But it's time. Sierra, I am going to move that we form a committee on trusteeship that recruits new board members and also nominates new officers. We've never had that, but it's time. Our mission requires it of us."

It was quiet—again. Michael took the gavel and then gave it back. "Phil, we each belong right where we are, but let's continue the conversation—maybe over wings at Anchors?"

Crystal was the last to leave that night. The table remained. The empty chair was no longer silent. It had a voice. In fact, it was as if each chair in that room was more conscious of the other. Crystal turned off the light, already looking forward to what next month would bring for City Farm—and to all of them.

A Boardroom Is Never Empty, a Table Resides

We have sought to offer practical capacity-building conversation starters for board members and their boards. At the center of our effort is a conviction that governance is a practice worthy of mastery. Governance is not a transactional volunteer role, considered complete if you have managed to get to most of the meetings, stayed awake and dropped a few coins in the tip jar so the staff can report to its grantors that "100% of our board members give." We raise the question as to when 100% board participation has been achieved. We assert: board service requires 100% readiness to be changed as we do the work of social change.

We chose a familiar symbol to organize focus on this conviction, the boardroom table. Culture, often described as an iceberg, has its observable features as well as its unseen dimension. Most everyone knows the *Titanic* did not sink because of what it could see above the surface of the waters. The danger lay below the waterline. Out of sight, out of mind. We turned the iceberg into a piece of furniture. We have sought to say: The boardroom is never empty. A table resides there. The table is a provocateur of our awareness, asking us to think deeply, beyond the surface. It invites us to speak deeply, to get it all out on the table.

Western thinking is prone to language games that treat the tangible, material, kickable world as the *real* world. Practical people, grounded people, seldom bother themselves with what they cannot see, touch or feel. Vaunting this incomplete education as knowledge, even as status, they excuse themselves from the social laws that govern as graciously as gravity, if you harness them. But gravity can be unforgiving. Those who ignore its laws are schooled through the consequences that follow. These consequences are true and forcible—despite being undetectable by the physical eye. Social laws can be unforgiving too, just as consequential as gravity when ignored.

Each member's connection to the mission deserves to be fanned into a flame such that their contribution to board service allows them not only the opportunity to serve a cause that matters to them, but also an opportunity to be transformed as a social agent as they do. Your board's culture can be an incubator for culture-shifting dispositions and culture-shifting conversations. Boards who make time to enter into a conversation about their unspoken agreements, undiscussable conflicts and unmentionable cultural questions engage in a vulnerable process that elevates the voices around their table and deepens their capacity to render unified governance service to their mission.

We bid you to take a deep gaze at the seat you occupy. With the subtle table ornament of a placemat, we boldly urge board members to claim their seats in humility, building trust with others, serving the common good by lifting their voice when missional imperatives call it forth.

Notes

Preface

1. Churchman, C. West, "Wicked Problems," *Management Science* 14 (4) (December 1967): B-141–B-146.

Introduction

2. *Collected Works of Mahatma Gandhi*, Volume XII, April 1913 to December 1914, Chapter: General Knowledge about Health XXXII: Accidents Snake-Bite (From Gujarati, Indian Opinion, 9-8-1913), Start Page 156, Quote Page 158, The Publications Division, Ministry of Information and Broadcasting, Government of India. (*Collected Works of Mahatma Gandhi* at gandhi heritageportal.org.)

3. McKinsey & Company, "Toward a Value-Creating Board," February 1, 2016, Survey. Accessed January 3, 2024. https://www.mckinsey.com /capabilities/strategy-and-corporate-finance/our-insights/toward-a-value -creating-board#/.

4. O'Kelley, Rusty, Rich Fields, Laura Sanderson, Beatrice Ballini, Margot McShane, Ryoko Komatsuzaki, Hans Roth, PJ Neal and Elena Loridas, "Inclusive Culture and DE&I: Gold Medal Boards Take the Lead," Russell Reynolds Associates, April 29, 2022. https://www.russellreynolds.com/en /insights/reports-surveys/global-board-culture-and-director-behaviors -study/inclusive-culture-and-dei.

Chapter 1

5. Kevin (last name protected), "My Cultural Identity Journey." Unpublished term paper, Asbury Seminary, 2003.

6. Du Bois, W. E. B., *The Souls of Black Folk* (New York: Penguin, 1903).

Chapter 2

7. Welty, Eudora, *One Time, One Place: Mississippi in the Depression: A Snapshot Album* (Jackson: University Press of Mississippi, 2002).

Chapter 3

8. David McCullough Quote, AZQuotes.com, Wind and Fly LTD. Accessed January 4, 2024. https://www.azquotes.com/quote/1350793.

Chapter 4

9. Frei, Frances X., and Anne Morriss, "Begin with Trust," *Harvard Business Review*, May 1, 2020. https://hbr.org/2020/05/begin-with-trust.

10. *2024 Edelman Trust Barometer*, Edelman. Accessed January 4, 2024. www.edelman.com/trust/2024/trust-barometer.

11. Allport, Gordon W., *The Nature of Prejudice* (Cambridge, MA: Perseus Books, 1954).

12. Janis, Irving, *Victims of Groupthink* (New York: Houghton Mifflin, 1972).

13. Rae, Aparna, "DEI Fatigue: Resistance or Opportunity? Unpacking This Moment and Navigating the Path Forward," *Forbes*, August 17, 2023. https://www.forbes.com/sites/aparnarae/2023/08/17/dei-fatigue-resistance-or-opportunity-unpacking-this-moment-and-navigating-the-path-forward/. For further discussion on this topic, see Zheng, Lily, *DEI Deconstructed: Your No-Nonsense Guide to Doing the Work and Doing It Right* (Oakland, CA: Berrett-Koehler, 2023).

14. Oshry, Barry, *Seeing Systems: Unlocking the Mysteries of Organizational Life* (San Francisco: Berrett-Koehler, 1995).

15. Rodopman, Burcu, "AES Corporation—Serving People and Society," in *Humanistic Management in Practice*, ed. Ernst von Kimakowitz, Michael Pirson, Heiko Spitzeck, Claus Dierksmeier and Wolfgang Amann (London: Palgrave Macmillan UK, 2011), 28–41.

16. See Crandall, Doug, and Matt Kincaid, *Permission to Speak Freely: How the Best Leaders Cultivate a Culture of Candor* (Oakland, CA: Berrett-Koehler, 2017).

Chapter 5

17. Frost, Robert, "Mending Wall," in *North of Boston* (Portland, ME: Mint Editions, 2021).

18. Jukanovich, Jennifer M., "A Conceptual Framework for How Trust and Humility Inform the Perception of Leadership among Rwandan Cooperative Members" (2022). *Theses and Dissertations*. 1302. https://digitalcommons.pepperdine.edu/etd/1302.

19. "What Are the Two Ways to Fail? Hear from Barry Rowan—Speaker, Leader, Trustee at Gordon College and Author of *The Spiritual Art of Business: Connecting...*: By Gordon College." Facebook, Gordon College, October 18, 2023. www.facebook.com/watch/?v=2047514925610095.

20. Schein, Edgar H., *Humble Leadership: The Power of Relationships, Openness, and Trust* (Oakland, CA: Berrett-Koehler, 2023).

21. Rovelli, Paola, and Camilla Curnis, "The Perks of Narcissism: Behaving Like a Star Speeds up Career Advancement to the CEO Position," *The Leadership Quarterly*, 32 (3) (December 11, 2020). https://doi.org/10.1016/j.leaqua.2020.101489.

22. Porath, Christine, "Make Civility the Norm on Your Team," *Harvard Business Review*, April 3, 2018. https://hbr.org/2018/01/make-civility-the-norm-on-your-team.

23. Lewis Faulk, Mirae Kim, Teresa Derrick-Mills, Elizabeth Boris, Laura Tomasko, and Nora Hakizimana, "National Findings on Diversity and Representation in the Nonprofit Sector: Nonprofit Trends and Impacts 2021," The Urban Institute. November, 2021. Accessed: January 4, 2024. https://www.urban.org/sites/default/files/2021/11/05/national_findings_on_diversity_and_representation_in_the_nonprofit_sector.pdf

24. Van Bommel, Tara, "The Power of Empathy in Times of Crisis and

Beyond," September 14, 2021. https://www.catalyst.org/reports/empathy
-work-strategy-crisis.

25. West, Russell, "Annie Ruth" (pseudonym), personal videotaped
interview, December 20, 2023. Used by permission.

26. Lewis, John, Public address at Edmund Pettus Bridge in Selma,
Alabama, on March 1, 2020. https://www.cnn.com/2020/03/01/politics/john
-lewis-bloody-sunday-march-selma/index.html.

Chapter 6

27. Johnson, James Weldon, "Lift Every Voice and Sing," in *Complete
Poems* (2000) (Washington, DC: Library of Congress). Accessed January 4,
2024. https://www.loc.gov/item/89751755/.

28. Reynolds, Marcia, *Coach the Person, Not the Problem: A Guide to Using
Reflective Inquiry* (Oakland, CA: Berrett-Koehler, 2020).

29. Boston Consulting Group, Questions, Boston Consulting Group
study. https://www.bcg.com/capabilities/organization/organizational-culture.

Chapter 7

30. Taylor, "102 Incredibly Wise Lao Tzu Leadership Quotes," Imperfect
Taylor, March 21, 2023. Accessed March 13, 2024. https://imperfecttaylor
.com/lao-tzu-leadership-quotes/.

31. Lewis, C. S., *Surprised by Joy* (New York: Harcourt Brace and Company, 1955), 207–208.

32. Henderson, Silas, "On Serving 'Because We Are Catholic, not Because They Are,'" Aleteia, July 2019. Accessed January 3, 2024. https://aleteia
.org/2019/07/13/on-serving-because-we-are-catholic-not-because-they-are/.

33. Corporate reputation is increasingly being measured, as it often
impacts other indicators of employee retention, branding and performance.
Board composition and board diversity are also seen as indicators of good
governance. For further reading on this, examine García-Meca, Emma,
and Carlos Palacio, "Board Composition and Firm Reputation: The Role
of Business Experts, Support Specialists and Community Influentials,"
Business Research Quarterly, February 27, 2018. https://www.sciencedirect
.com/science/article/pii/S2340943618300331.

34. Queenan, Jeri Eckhart, Peter Grunert and Devin Murphy, "Elevating the Role of Faith-Inspired Impact in the Social Sector," Bridgespan, January 28, 2021. Accessed November 5, 2023. https://www.bridgespan.org/insights /role-of-faith-inspired-impact-in-the-social-sector.

Chapter 8

35. Murdoch, Iris, Essay in *The Sovereignty of Good* (London: Routledge & Kegan Paul, 1970), 37.

36. Siegel, Robert, and Art Silverman, "During World War I, U.S. Government Propaganda Erased German Culture," NPR, April 7, 2017. www.npr .org/2017/04/07/523044253/during-world-war-i-u-s-government-propaganda -erased-german-culture.

37. Beihl, Bobb, and Ted Engstrom, *The Effective Board Member: Secrets of Making a Significant Contribution to Any Organization You Serve* (Nashville, TN: B & H Publishing Group, 1998).

Chapter 9

38. Bowen, Murray, "Postgraduate Program in Bowen Family Systems Theory and Its Applications," Bowen Center for the Study of the Family. Accessed January 3, 2024. https://www.thebowencenter.org/postgraduate -program.

39. Ong, Walter J., *Orality and Literacy: The Technologizing of the Word* (London: Routledge, 1996). In this book, Father Ong makes the historic divide between orality and technology cultures. The dispute in this scene has been played out throughout communication technology history. As early as the technology shift from chirography (handwriting) as the first displacement of orality in Plato's time, the group being superseded has always been defined by those whose privilege and purse allowed them to "advance," and then from that privileged position, the winner has defined "civilization" or who is civilized. The technological divide and the suspicions it awakens between haves and have-nots account for recurring intergroup anxiety in each era.

Chapter 10

40. Weil, Simone, *Need for Roots* (New York: Penguin, 2021).

41. Terry, Robert, *Seven Zones for Leadership: Acting Authentically in Stability and Chaos* (Palo Alto, CA: Davies-Black, 2001). Robert Terry discusses the "paradox of leadership" in this book.

42. Goldsmith, Daene J., "Puzzles in the Study of Enacted Social Support," in *Communicating Social Support, Advances in Personal Relationships* (Cambridge, UK: Cambridge University Press, 2004): 10–24; Kramer, Julia, "The Problem with 'Help' in Global Development," *Stanford Social Innovation Review*, September 3, 2015. https://doi.org/10.48558/23N2-E492.

Chapter 11

43. Den Heijer, Alexander, *Nothing You Don't Already Know: Remarkable Reminders about Meaning, Purpose and Self-Realization.* (Scotts Valley, CA: CreateSpace Independent Publishing Platform, 2018).

Works Cited

Achebe, Chinua, *Things Fall Apart* (London: Penguin Classics, 2006).

Allport, Gordon W., *The Nature of Prejudice* (Cambridge, MA: Perseus Books, 1954).

Beihl, Bobb, and Ted Engstrom, *The Effective Board Member: Secrets of Making a Significant Contribution to Any Organization You Serve* (Nashville, TN: B & H Publishing Group, 1998).

Boston Consulting Group, Questions, Boston Consulting Group study. Accessed January 4, 2024. https://www.bcg.com/capabilities/organization-strategy/organizational-culture. .

Bowen, Murray, "Postgraduate Program in Bowen Family Systems Theory and Its Applications," Bowen Center for the Study of the Family. Accessed January 3, 2024. https://www.thebowencenter.org/postgraduate-program.

Burdick, Eugene, and William Lederer, *The Ugly American* (New York: Norton, 1958).

Churchman, C. West, *Management Science* 14 (4) (December 1967): B-141–B-146.

Collected Works of Mahatma Gandhi, Volume XII, April 1913 to December 1914, Chapter: General Knowledge about Health XXXII: Accidents Snake-Bite (From Gujarati, Indian Opinion, 9-8-1913), Start Page 156, Quote Page 158, The Publications Division, Ministry of Information and Broadcasting, Government of India. (*Collected Works of Mahatma Gandhi* at gandhiheritageportal.org.)

Crandall, Doug, and Matt Kincaid, *Permission to Speak Freely: How the Best Leaders Cultivate a Culture of Candor* (Oakland, CA: Berrett-Koehler, 2017).

David McCullough Quote, AZQuotes.com, Wind and Fly LTD. Accessed January 4, 2024. https://www.azquotes.com/quote/1350793.

Den Heijer, Alexander, *Nothing You Don't Already Know: Remarkable Reminders about Meaning, Purpose and Self-Realization* (Scotts Valley, CA: CreateSpace Independent Publishing Platform, 2018).

Du Bois, W. E. B., *The Souls of Black Folk* (New York: Penguin, 1903).

Frei, X., and Anne Morriss, "Begin with Trust," *Harvard Business Review.* May 1, 2020. https://hbr.org/2020/05/begin-with-trust.

Frost, Robert, "Mending Wall," in *North of Boston* (Portland, ME: Mint Editions, 2021).

García-Meca, Emma, and Carlos Palacio, "Board Composition and Firm Reputation: The Role of Business Experts, Support Specialists and Community Influentials," *BRQ Business Research Quarterly.* February 27, 2018. https://www.sciencedirect.com/science/article/pii/S2340943618300331.

Henderson, Silas, "On Serving 'Because We Are Catholic, not Because They Are,'" Aleteia, July 2019. Accessed January 3, 2024. https://aleteia .org/2019/07/13/on-serving-because-we-are-catholic-not-because-they -are/.

Janis, Irving, *Victims of Groupthink* (New York: Houghton Mifflin, 1972).

Johnson, James Weldon, "Lift Every Voice and Sing," in *Complete Poems* (Washington, DC: Library of Congress, 2000). Accessed January 4, 2024. https://www.loc.gov/item/89751755/.

Jukanovich, Jennifer M., "A Conceptual Framework for How Trust and Humility Inform the Perception of Leadership among Rwandan Cooperative Members" (2022). *Theses and Dissertations.* 1302. https://digitalcommons .pepperdine.edu/etd/1302.

Kevin (last name protected), "My Cultural Identity Journey." Unpublished term paper, Asbury Seminary, 2003.

Kingsolver, Barbara, *Poisonwood Bible* (London: Faber and Faber, 2000).

Lewis, C. S., *Surprised by Joy* (Harcourt Brace and Company, 1955), 207–208.

Lewis, John, Public address at Edmund Pettus Bridge in Selma, Alabama, on March 1, 2020, CNN. March 3, 2020. https://www.cnn.com/2020/03/01/ politics/john-lewis-bloody-sunday-march-selma/index.html.

McKinsey & Company, "Toward a Value-Creating Board," February 1, 2016, Survey. Accessed January 3, 2024. https://www.mckinsey.com/

capabilities/strategy-and-corporate-finance/our-insights/toward-a-value
-creating-board#/.

Murdoch, Iris, Essay in *The Sovereignty of Good* (London: Routledge & Kegan
Paul, 1970), 37.

O'Kelley, Rusty, Rich Fields, Laura Sanderson, Beatrice Ballini, Margot
McShane, Ryoko Komatsuzaki, Hans Roth, PJ Neal and Elena Loridas,
"Inclusive Culture and DE&I: Gold Medal Boards Take the Lead," Russell
Reynolds Associates. April 29, 2022. https://www.russellreynolds.com/
en/insights/reports-surveys/global-board-culture-and-director-behaviors
-study/inclusive-culture-and-dei.

Ong, Walter J., *Orality and Literacy: The Technologizing of the Word* (London:
Routledge, 1996).

Porath, Christine, "Make Civility the Norm on Your Team," *Harvard
Business Review.* April 3, 2018. https://hbr.org/2018/01/make-civility-the
-norm-on-your-team.

Queenan, Jeri Eckhart, Peter Grunert and Devin Murphy, "Elevating
the Role of Faith-Inspired Impact in the Social Sector," Bridgespan.
Accessed November 5, 2023. https://www.bridgespan.org/insights/
role-of-faith-inspired-impact-in-the-social-sector.

Rae, Aparna, "DEI Fatigue: Resistance or Opportunity? Unpacking This Moment and Navigating the Path Forward," *Forbes.* August 17, 2023. https://
www.forbes.com/sites/aparnarae/2023/08/17/dei-fatigue-resistance-or
-opportunity-unpacking-this-moment-and-navigating-the-path-forward/
?sh=15557ac355af.

Reynolds, Marcia, *Coach the Person, Not the Problem: A Guide to Using Reflective Inquiry* (Oakland, CA: Berrett-Koehler, 2020).

Robert, M. Henry, *Robert's Pocket Manual of Rules of Order for Deliberative
Assemblies* (Chicago, New York: Scott, Foresman and Company, 1896).

Rodopman, Burcu, "AES Corporation—Serving People and Society," in
Humanistic Management in Practice, ed. Ernst von Kimakowitz, Michael
Pirson, Heiko Spitzeck, Claus Dierksmeier and Wolfgang Amann (Lon-
don: Palgrave Macmillan UK, 2011), 28–41.

Rovelli, Paola, et al., "The Perks of Narcissism: Behaving like a Star Speeds
up Career Advancement to the CEO Position," *The Leadership Quarterly,*
JAI. December 11, 2020. www.sciencedirect.com/science/article/abs/pii/
S1048984320301168.

Schein, Edgar H., *Humble Leadership: The Power of Relationships, Openness, and Trust* (Oakland, CA: Berrett-Koehler, 2023).

Siegel, Robert, and Art Silverman, "During World War I, U.S. Government Propaganda Erased German Culture," NPR. April 7, 2017. www.npr.org/2017/04/07/523044253/during-world-war-i-u-s-government-propaganda-erased-german-culture.

Taylor, "102 Incredibly Wise Lao Tzu Leadership Quotes," Imperfect Taylor, March 21, 2023. Accessed January 3, 2024. https://imperfecttaylor.com/lao-tzu-leadership-quotes.

Terry, Robert, *Seven Zones for Leadership: Acting Authentically in Stability and Chaos* (Palo Alto, CA: Davies-Black, 2001).

2024 Edelman Trust Barometer, Edelman. January 14, 2024. www.edelman.com/trust/2024/trustbarometer.

Van Bommel, T., "The Power of Empathy in Times of Crisis and Beyond." September 14, 2021. https://www.catalyst.org/reports/empathy-work-strategy-crisis.

Weil, Simone, *Need for Roots* (New York: Harper Collins, 1977).

Welty, Eudora, *One Time, One Place: Mississippi in the Depression: A Snapshot Album* (Jackson: University Press of Mississippi, 2002).

West, Russell, "Annie Ruth" (pseudonym), personal videotaped interview, December 20, 2023. Used by permission.

"What Are the Two Ways to Fail? Hear from Barry Rowan—Speaker, Leader, Trustee at Gordon College and Author of *The Spiritual Art of Business: Connecting…: By Gordon College.*" Facebook, Gordon College. October 18, 2023. www.facebook.com/watch/?v=2047514925610095.

Zheng, Lily, *DEI Deconstructed: Your No-Nonsense Guide to Doing the Work and Doing It Right* (Oakland, CA: Berrett-Koehler, 2023).

Acknowledgments

We extend our heartfelt gratitude to the colleagues whose unwavering support made this book possible. First and foremost, thanks to our colleagues at the M.J. Murdock Charitable Trust: to Kimberly Thornbury, who saw it first and said, "This may be more than a training module, might be a book"; retired CEO and personal mentor, Steve Moore, for his encouragement; Romanita Hairston, Murdock's inspiring leader, who believed in the power of this book to help build islands of sanctuary in the social transformation sector; our fellow coaches, Bob, Ron, Greg, Ed and Deborah. We are grateful for their wisdom, example and invaluable guidance throughout the publication process. Additionally, we extend our sincere thanks to the many boards on which we serve and have coached, those who continually seek to make the world a better place. Sometimes our conversations are hard, but you remain at the table and have taught us both so much.

We are indebted to Neal Maillet at Berrett-Koehler for taking a risk and believing in the message of this book and to his incredible team for their expertise, encouragement and dedication in shaping this manuscript into its final form. Their mission to connect people and ideas that creates a world that works for all inspires us. Matt and Doug, thank you for your incredible counsel that first led us to BK.

Jennifer would like to thank: Dano, my husband of 27 years, thank you for always encouraging my dreams, making the sacrifices to see them happen and growing with me on this journey; my children, Lian,

Anna and Nathanael, you are my *why*, I can't imagine our family story without you, and thank you for your patience and encouragement during all the late nights of writing; Mom, thank you for modeling an open table that welcomed the stranger, inspiring in me a love for hospitality and pushing me out the door to learn from other cultures; for my dad, thank you for teaching me the power of storytelling, and I wish you were here to read this; and my extended family, Marko, Shelley, Jon and Amy, for your constant love and encouragement. To my friends and family around the globe who humble me with their encouragement and inspiration, I am grateful: Abby and Suzanne, for making me stop in the middle of the Camino de Santiago last September to write down my book ideas; Lisa and Kirsten who kept the writing process real for me with your wisdom; Brook and Susan who prayed these words would find a home; my Gordon Gals, for a lifetime of encouragement; my Pepperdine Ph.D. cohort who model staying at the table for the greater good; JR, for asking the right questions this year; and Bob, for teaching me why board governance matters.

Russ would like to thank: Mom and Dad, Mildred and (the late) Ralph West, who both taught me the first word of cultural consciousness, a breathless "Wow" as I absorb the variegated beauty of cultural strangers. My dearest Lorin, you are my favorite people-watcher. Thank you for the street-level view you brought to the conversation. Josh, I'm so impressed how you embody and model to me daily the spiritual generosity toward self and others, so necessary for any of this book's promises to be realized, doing so without even breaking a sweat. Liam, most likely, you will be a board chair one day. Bobb Beihl, mentor and friend, you have inspired my own boardroom confidence and that of thousands since that first board meeting in '92. Sara Huron, my editorial coach, thank you for the unwavering belief that fragments, lived and written, honor the moments when we are most awake. Rebecca, my world's most provocative coach, there are hardly words…and that, we know, is testimony you have been here. Janet, your penetrative simplicity awakens me to the subtleties in organizational service. Izzie, encouragement is a verb because of you. Kevin and Jonathan, thank you for the companionship in the "slow and low" way. Ray, thank you for decades in which organizational spirituality never left our table talk since the first start-up. Last, to the memory of my colleague and college roomie, Paul Litten: you were the sailboat that came by, and you took me *with* you.

We are grateful to each for their unwavering support and understanding during the curation of this book.

Thank you all for being part of this journey.

Jennifer M. Jukanovich, PhD
Russell W. West, PhD

Index

About the Authors

JARED CHARNEY

Jennifer M. Jukanovich, PhD   Jennifer brings 25 years of international and domestic nonprofit leadership and board experience to her role as Managing Partner of Ambactus Global Solutions, which harnesses the power of connection to solve complex problems in governance, international development and education. She actively works with a diverse range of nonprofit clients, such as artists doing community development for children and refugees, scientists and scholars cultivating human flourishing, educators in the United States and Africa seeking new pathways of learning and those accompanying survivors of prostitution to heal from gender-based violence. In addition, she serves as a coach and faculty for the M.J. Murdock Charitable Trust and as a co-investigator for the internationally celebrated 2020 GLOBE (Global Leadership and Organizational Behavior Effectiveness) project. She served as Vice President for Student Life at Gordon College from 2013 to 2019. Prior to this, Jukanovich lived and worked in Rwanda, where her family co-founded Karisimbi Business Partners, a management consulting and private equity firm. She has also held positions as the Founder and Executive Director of The Vine, executive assistant to the president of the Council for Christian Colleges and Universities, personal assistant to the religious liaison for the President of the United States and as an associate with the Renaissance Weekends. She has her PhD in Global Leadership and Change from Pepperdine University, Master's in Theology from Fuller Theological Seminary and a BA in Political Studies from Gordon College. Jennifer serves on several nonprofit boards and lives with her family in the Boston area.

 **Russell W. West, PhD**   For three decades, West has held multiple roles, including college president, dean, professor, nonprofit impact strategist, executive coach and even Marine drill instructor for Officers Candidates. Professionally, Russ is a certified executive and organizational performance coach, supporting C-suite decision-making at Geisinger Healthcare in Danville, Pennsylvania, and Advent Health in Florida in both acute and non-acute locations. He is a member of the M.J. Murdock Charitable Trust's Non-Profit Leader's enrichment program, where he works with Jennifer in their *Culture 201* experience. He serves on Kellogg School of Management's Non-Profit Executive Coaching Faculty and lectures in Buffalo University's Business School's executive coaching program. West has founded/co-founded three nonprofits and engaged in nonprofit board and strategy consultancy since 2004, assisting numerous nonprofit/ small businesses. Known for his deep listening, strategic thinking and fostering of positive change in teams, West excels in cultivating empathic work teams driving significant social impact. In his spare time, he enjoys family, horse work and sailing.

Berrett–Koehler
Publishers

Berrett-Koehler is an independent publisher dedicated to an ambitious mission: *Connecting people and ideas to create a world that works for all.*

Our publications span many formats, including print, digital, audio, and video. We also offer online resources, training, and gatherings. And we will continue expanding our products and services to advance our mission.

We believe that the solutions to the world's problems will come from all of us, working at all levels: in our society, in our organizations, and in our own lives. Our publications and resources offer pathways to creating a more just, equitable, and sustainable society. They help people make their organizations more humane, democratic, diverse, and effective (and we don't think there's any contradiction there). And they guide people in creating positive change in their own lives and aligning their personal practices with their aspirations for a better world.

And we strive to practice what we preach through what we call "The BK Way." At the core of this approach is *stewardship,* a deep sense of responsibility to administer the company for the benefit of all of our stakeholder groups, including authors, customers, employees, investors, service providers, sales partners, and the communities and environment around us. Everything we do is built around stewardship and our other core values of *quality, partnership, inclusion,* and *sustainability.*

This is why Berrett-Koehler is the first book publishing company to be both a B Corporation (a rigorous certification) and a benefit corporation (a for-profit legal status), which together require us to adhere to the highest standards for corporate, social, and environmental performance. And it is why we have instituted many pioneering practices (which you can learn about at www.bkconnection.com), including the Berrett-Koehler Constitution, the Bill of Rights and Responsibilities for BK Authors, and our unique Author Days.

We are grateful to our readers, authors, and other friends who are supporting our mission. We ask you to share with us examples of how BK publications and resources are making a difference in your lives, organizations, and communities at www.bkconnection.com/impact.

Dear reader,

Thank you for picking up this book and welcome to the worldwide BK community! You're joining a special group of people who have come together to create positive change in their lives, organizations, and communities.

What's BK all about?

Our mission is to connect people and ideas to create a world that works for all.

Why? Our communities, organizations, and lives get bogged down by old paradigms of self-interest, exclusion, hierarchy, and privilege. But we believe that can change. That's why we seek the leading experts on these challenges—and share their actionable ideas with you.

A welcome gift

To help you get started, we'd like to offer you a **free copy** of one of our bestselling ebooks:

www.bkconnection.com/welcome

When you claim your **free ebook**, you'll also be subscribed to our blog.

Our freshest insights

Access the best new tools and ideas for leaders at all levels on our blog at ideas.bkconnection.com.

Sincerely,

Your friends at Berrett-Koehler

Certified

Corporation